Sequoyah

AND THE CHEROKEE ALPHABET

Alvin Josephy's Biography Series of American Indians

Sequoyah

AND THE CHEROKEE ALPHABET

Written by Robert Cwiklik

INTRODUCTION BY ALVIN M. JOSEPHY, JR.
ILLUSTRATED BY T. LEWIS

Project editors: Nancy Furstinger (Silver Burdett Press)
Mark Davies & Della Rowland (Kipling Press)
Designed by Mike Hortens

This edition published June 2000 by Sonlight Curriculum, Ltd., by
permission of Pearson Learning, an imprint of Pearson Education, Inc.,
successor-in-interest to Silver Burdett Press.

Printed in the United States of America.

10 9 8 7 6 5 4 3 2 1 (Lib. ed.)
10 9 8 7 6 5   (Pbk. ed.)

Library of Congress Cataloging-in-Publication Data

Cwiklik, Robert.
Sequoyah and the Cherokee Alphabet / by Robert Cwiklik :
Introduction by Alvin M. Josephy, Jr. : illustrations by T. Lewis.
p. cm.—(Alvin Josephy's biography series of American Indians)
Bibliography: p. 130
Summary: A biography of the Cherokee Indian who invented a method
for his people to write and read their own language.
1. Sequoyah, 1770?-1843—Juvenile literature. 2. Cherokee
Indians—Biography—Juvenile literature. 3. Indians of North
America—Southern States—Biography—Juvenile literature.
4. Cherokee Indians—Writing—Juvenile literature. 5. Indians of
North America—Southern States—Writing—Juvenile literature.
[1. Sequoyah, 1770?-1843. 2. Cherokee Indians—Biography.
3. Indians of North America—Southern States—Biography.]
I. Lewis, T. (Thomas), ill.   II. Title.   III. Series.
E99. C5S3823   1989   89-30737
975'.00497—dc19   CIP
[B]   AC
ISBN 0-382-09570-7 (lib. bdg.)
ISBN 0-382-09759-9 (pbk.)

Contents

Although this book is based on real events and real people, some dialogue, a few thoughts, and several local descriptions have been reconstructed to make the story more enjoyable. It does not, however, alter the basic truth of the story we are telling.

Unless indicated otherwise, the Indian designs used throughout this book are purely decorative, and do not signify a particular tribe or nation.

∞   ∞   ∞

Introduction

For 500 years, Christopher Columbus has been hailed as the "discoverer" of America. But Columbus only discovered America for his fellow Europeans, who did not know of its existence. America was really discovered more than 10,000 years before the time of Columbus by people who came across the Bering Strait from Siberia into Alaska. From there they spread south to populate both North and South America. By the time of Columbus, in fact, there were millions of descendants of the true discoverers of America living in all parts of the Western Hemisphere. They inhabited the territory from the northern shores of Alaska and Canada to the southern tip of South America. In what is now the United States, hundreds of tribes, large and small, covered the land from Maine and Florida to Puget Sound and California. Each tribe had a long and proud history of its own.

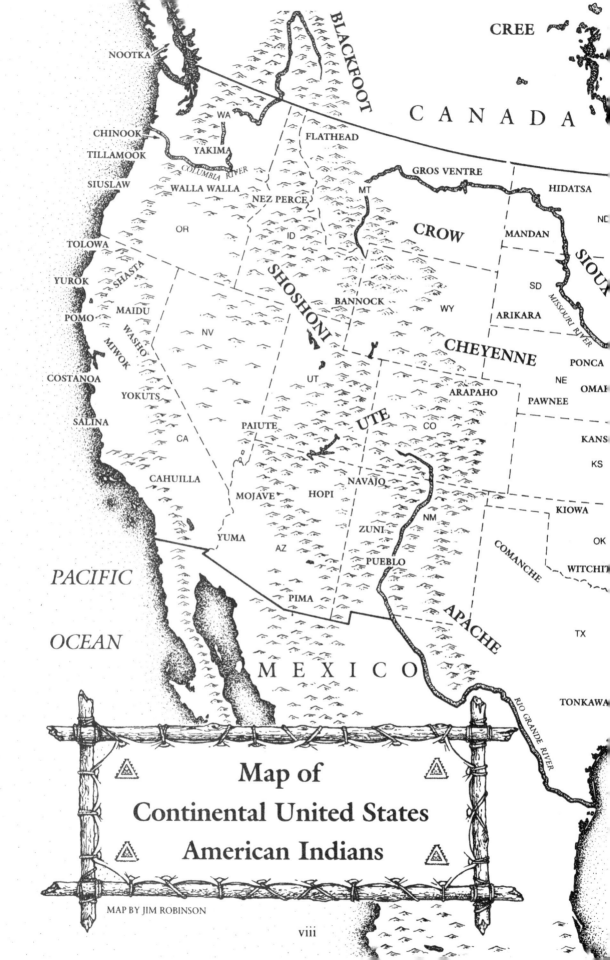

Map of
Continental United States
American Indians

MAP BY JIM ROBINSON

America was hardly an "unknown world," an "unexplored wilderness"—except to the Europeans who gazed for the first time upon its forests and rivers, its prairies and mountains.

From the very beginning, the newcomers from Europe had many mistaken notions about the people whose ancestors had been living in America for centuries. At first Columbus thought he had reached the East Indies of Asia, and he called the people Indians. The name took hold and remains to this day. But there were more serious misconceptions that had a tragic effect on relations between the Indians and the Europeans. These misconceptions led to one of the greatest holocausts in world history. Indians were robbed of their possessions, their lands, and the lives of countless numbers of their people.

Most Europeans never really understood the thinking, beliefs, values, or religions of the Indians. The Indian way of life was so different from that of the Europeans, who had inherited thousands of years of diverse backgrounds, religions, and ways of thinking and acting. The Europeans looked down on the Indians as strange and different, and therefore inferior. They were ignorant in the way they treated the Indians. To the white people, the Indians were "savages" and "barbarians," who either had to change their ways and become completely like the Europeans or be destroyed.

At the same time, many Europeans came as conquerors. They wanted the Indians' lands and the resources of those lands—resources such as gold, silver, and furs. Their greed, their superior weapons, and their contempt for the Indians' "inferior" ways led to many wars. Of course the Indians fought back to protect the lives of their people, their lands, their religions, their freedoms, their very way of life. But the Europeans—and then their American descendants—assumed that the Indians were all fierce warriors who fought simply because they loved to fight. Only in recent years have we come to see the Indians as they really are—people who would fight when their lives and freedom were at stake. People who were fun-loving children, young lovers, mothers who cried for the safety and health of their families, fathers who did their best to provide food, wise old people who gave advice, religious leaders, philosophers, statesmen, artists, musicians, storytellers, makers of crafts. Yes, and scientists, engineers, and builders of cities as well. The Indian civilizations in Mexico and Peru were among the most advanced the world has ever known.

This book gets beneath the surface of the old, worn-out fables to tell a real story of the Indians—to help us understand how the Indians looked at the world. When we understand this, we can see not only what they did, but why they did it. Everything here is accurate history, and it is an exciting story. And it is told in such a way that we, the readers, can imagine ourselves back among the Indians of the past, identifying ourselves with their ways of life, beliefs, and destinies. Perhaps in the end we will be able to ask: What choices would we have had? How would we ourselves have responded and behaved?

Sequoyah was both a remarkable man and a member of a remarkable tribe. The Cherokees were powerful, numerous, and intelligent. They had every kind of pressure put on them to

Cherokee syllabary

abandon their Indian way of life and become like white people. The pressure put upon them caused terrible conflict and disagreements within the tribe. Eventually, though, large numbers of Cherokees found ways to accept what they felt was useful to them in the white person's world; and at the same time they kept what they wished of their old traditional Cherokee culture.

In a way, Sequoyah's great achievement—the invention of a method for his people to write and read their own language—was a symbol of this adjustment. This great leader was celebrated not as a warrior, but as a man of ideas. Today, a statue of Sequoyah stands in the Capitol building in Washington, D.C. He is a truly outstanding example of an Indian who made his mark on history. To all Americans, he is an inspiring and unforgettable figure.

—Alvin M. Josephy, Jr.

1
A Sublime Skull

A well-dressed man in a topcoat and hat walked along a busy side street in downtown Washington, D.C. It was a midsummer afternoon in the year 1835. The stench of sewage from the swamp by the White House was almost unbearable. The man tapped his cane on the sidewalk impatiently as he walked along inspecting the shop windows. He found the one he wanted. The hand-painted sign on the window read: "O.J. Fowlerhouse: Practical Phrenologist."

The bell on the door tinkled as the man entered and removed his hat. He was stocky, with ruddy cheeks, a broad forehead, a large nose, and clear eyes. He was noticed immediately.

"Ah, you must be Mister, er, ah, *Chief* Ross," said Mr. Fowlerhouse, who stood behind the counter. He was hunched over a white plaster model of a human head, which sat atop a pedestal on the countertop. He held a pencil, which he was using to draw lines on the plaster head, dividing its surface into sections.

"Yes, I am Chief Ross. Now, please, be quick about this. I have many matters of pressing business."

The chief was not exaggerating. He was in Washington to visit the president of the United States and some members of Congress. The government had plans to remove his tribe, the Cherokee

Indians, from their homeland in the southeast United States. Many wanted to force the Cherokees to move to the wild, barren lands west of the Mississippi River—what they called Indian Territory. Congressmen said that honest settlers of the Southeast couldn't be expected to live next to "savages," which is what they felt the Indians were. But if they could have seen this Cherokee chief, they might have felt differently. There he stood in his pressed black suit and buffed riding boots, the picture of a country gentleman.

"Yes, yes, we shall proceed directly," said Mr. Fowlerhouse. He was a slight, baldheaded man, with pince-nez glasses tied to his ears by a leather cord. "Yes, yes, yes," he said. "Well, Mr. Ross, I mean Chief Ross, I should like to help you prove to those nincompoops in the Congress that you and your, er, kind are not inferior beings at all. No, sir, not inferior at all, neither morally nor intellectually." He pushed his glasses back on his nose with a huff. The chief pulled out his pocket watch and glanced hard at it. Mr. Fowlerhouse knew this man would be a difficult sale.

Mr. Fowlerhouse was a phrenologist. Phrenologists are people who study skulls. In the nineteenth century many of them believed that the shape of a person's head determined how intelligent or even how moral that person was. Mr. Fowlerhouse was hoping to get a little free publicity by selling his services as a phrenologist to the Cherokees, whose cause was becoming very famous in the United States.

To convince Chief Ross to hire him, Mr. Fowlerhouse had prepared a plaster model of the head of a man from the chief's tribe. The man's name was Sequoyah. He was already one of the most famous Indians in the country. In fact, accounts of his achievement had spread around the world.

Sequoyah had invented a way for the Cherokees to write down their language. Up to this time, they had only been able to *speak* their language. Sequoyah had created a syllabary, which is very much like an alphabet. A syllabary is a set of written symbols, or characters, like the letters of an alphabet. However, each character in a syllabary represents a syllable of a word. In an alphabet, each character stands for one letter only.

Sequoyah is the only person in history ever to invent an entire writing system single-handedly. Because of his syllabary, the Cherokee were the first North American Indian tribe to have a written language. So it is understandable why the newspapers made such a fuss over him, and why a certain phrenologist took—or said he took—an impression of Sequoyah's head when the famous Indian visited Washington in 1828. Everyone was curious about this "Indian genius."

"Very well," said Chief Ross with a wave of his hand, "proceed."

The phrenologist put his hands on the model head. "I took the liberty of making this plaster cast of your, er, fellow tribesman when he was last in our city—the man they call Sequoyah. He's the clever fellow who invented your Cherokee alphabet. That really was a good job, wasn't it?"

"It's not an alphabet, it's a syllabary," Chief Ross corrected.

"Yes, of course it is," Mr. Fowlerhouse puffed. "But it really doesn't matter. You see, this model I've done of his head shows that you Cherokees are not an ounce inferior to white men. Look here," he said, pointing to a lump in the skull near the temple. "This section is the seat of Sequoyah's, er, *sublimity*. It's rather large, wouldn't you say?"

"Mr. Fowlerhouse, I really don't think . . ." Chief Ross said impatiently.

"Now, just a moment," the phrenologist said. "Here," he continued, pointing to another bulge. "This very large section corresponds to Sequoyah's *ideality*. Surely this will prove to those barbarians in Congress that the Indian's intelligence is equal to the white man's."

The phrenologist cleared his throat and smiled wanly at Chief Ross.

"Mr. Fowlerhouse," Chief Ross said gravely, putting on his hat to leave, "I'm sure this doesn't prove anything. Furthermore, someone is sure to point out that even if Sequoyah is especially gifted, it is only because he is half-white."

"No!" exclaimed the phrenologist. "Half-white? I never heard . . ."

"It was in all the papers," said Chief Ross. "They say Sequoyah's father was a man named Nathanial Gist. You may have heard of him. He was a rich man, and a close friend of President Washington. Served with him in the war."

"Well, that would explain a lot," said Mr. Fowlerhouse. "To be the son of such a fine, accomplished statesman. Why, that must be where Sequoyah gets it from. I mean, it could be, couldn't it?" The phrenologist dropped his hands away from the model skull and sighed.

"I'm afraid it's not so simple," Chief Ross answered. "You see, Sequoyah was born more than fifty years ago. Cherokees at that time didn't keep birth records, and since Sequoyah's father left his mother before Sequoyah was born, no one is sure who the man was. Many think he was a white man named George Gist, not Nathanial Gist. The papers may have gotten the wrong Gist."

The phrenologist snickered. "Didn't get the Gist, that is good," he said.

"Yes, but the real joke is this George Gist," the chief snapped. "He was a Dutchman, a trader. If he was Sequoyah's father, then people should forget the idea that Sequoyah gets his brilliance from his white blood, because George Gist was a drunk and a scamp. If Sequoyah inherited anything from George Gist, he had to grow out of it before he could make anything of himself. Now, good day, sir. I have business."

Chief Ross walked out. The bell tinkled again as he shut the door firmly behind him.

"Didn't get the Gist," the phrenologist snickered softly.

2

This Land Was Made for You and Me

In the spring of 1769, George Gist rode up a shady mountain trail in northwest Georgia. He was nearing the heart of "Indian country." He led two pack mules by a rope tied to his saddle-horn. Their packs were stuffed with Dutch tomahawks, cheap jewelery, and other things the Indians loved. Gist hoped to make a fortune selling these to what he considered "those dumb Indians."

Gist was riding deeper into Indian country than most traders cared to go. The nearest white settlement was more than a hundred miles away. But the risks were worth it. The Indians would pay him in valuable furs for mere trinkets and cheap glass beads. He could get good silver for the furs. The Indians were like children, thought Gist. He grinned, showing a gold-capped tooth.

Up ahead Gist saw a group of Cherokee hunters trotting quietly along another trail that crossed his. They were dressed in buckskin vests and leggings. Their heads were shaved, except for a thin band of hair down the middle, and some wore a single feather in their hair. Each had a bow and arrows strapped to his back. They paid no attention to the trader. Indians traveled through the forest this way when they didn't have enough horses, which was most of the time. They would run for miles to their hunting grounds.

At a rocky ledge Gist stopped to look at the scenery. To the west, Lookout Mountain loomed up through the mist. Straight ahead were the rolling green hills of Tennessee. He was approaching the principal towns of the Cherokee nation.

As he rode on, Gist noticed smoke rising from a nearby village, where the hunters had come from. He thought of their families in this woodland nest. The women would be out hoeing and watering their crops, while their babies in cradleboards hung from the branches of trees or bushes.

He looked out dreamily over the vast forest, the spacious valley, and the rolling green hills, and remembered his own family. They had come here from Europe. They were looking for a better life, and they had found it on their Georgia farm. But the land in east Georgia was grabbed up quickly, and there were a lot more Europeans coming all the time—folks just like his family, looking for a new start.

He tried to imagine the thick forests ahead of him cut down and farmhouses standing in the midst of fields surrounded by acres of crops in neat rows. "Yup," he thought, "there's room for plenty more."

George Gist had forgotten one thing. The timberland he was mentally clearing for future settlers was already spoken for. It was the homeland of the Cherokees, who had lived there for hundreds of years.

It had been the same story over and over since Christopher Columbus first came to America in 1492. Europeans considered the vast continents of what are now North and South America their "New World," without caring if the Indians might have something to say about it.

When Columbus "discovered" America, the first thing he found out was that people already lived there. Columbus and his men came ashore on an island in the Bahamas, where they were warmly received by the native people. Columbus later wrote back to King Ferdinand and Queen Isabella of Spain, who had sponsored his voyage. He told them that the natives ". . . brought us parrots and balls of cotton and spears and many other things . . ." He described them as people who wore no clothing, and were well-built and healthy. Because they were friendly and generous, Columbus concluded that "with fifty men we could make them do whatever we want."

Columbus and the Spaniards did just that. They took prisoners among the people and brought them to Europe, displaying them like a circus act. Columbus called them "Indians," since he first thought he had reached the islands east of India, which were on the other side of the world. The name stuck, and afterward, all native people living in North and South America were called Indians by Europeans. But peoples often invent their own names for other groups of people. This is not a terrible crime. The terrible crimes followed.

Columbus and the Spaniards set out to make the Indians do "whatever we want." First they enslaved the Arawaks. The Arawaks were forced, with whips and swords, to do back-breaking toil in gold mines. The Spanish thought, wrongly, that their "New World" was rich in gold, and they were determined to get as much as they could. When their slaves couldn't find any, the gold-hungry Spaniards sometimes hacked the Arawaks' hands or arms off for refusing to give up the precious ore.

When the Arawaks resisted this treatment, there were wars. The natives were no match for the Spaniards and their muskets.

They were soon reduced to total enslavement. After a generation, the once carefree islanders were virtually wiped out.

Tragedies like this occurred almost everywhere the Europeans settled in the New World. The Indians always greeted the settlers warmly. When the earliest white settlers were starving, the Indians gave them food and taught them how to grow many crops, including tobacco, corn, tomatoes, and peanuts. The settlers eventually grew rich selling these same crops to Europeans. And as the settlements grew, they needed the Indians less and the Indians' land more.

Many of the Indians in North America were not as docile and helpless as the Arawaks. They fought fiercely, often killing women and children as well as men, to end the settlements on their lands once and for all. This fighting earned them the reputation of being "savages." But in the end, the story was always the same. The Indians were wiped out.

The Cherokee nation was inland, hundreds of miles from the Atlantic coast. But when the Dutch trader George Gist visited in 1769, the white settlers had already reached the borders of Cherokee territory. Earlier the Cherokees had given up some of their distant hunting grounds in Virginia and North Carolina to Europeans, but it seemed as if the white people always wanted more. As the white settlers advanced, the Indian nations fell like a row of dominoes, one after another. It looked like the Cherokees were the next in line.

The Europeans were seldom bothered by the disappearance of whole tribes of Indians. It didn't matter that the Indians' ancestors had lived on these lands for thousands of years before Europeans "discovered" them. The Europeans were "civilizing" the new world. The Indians were "savages," and there was no place for them.

Some well-meaning white people tried to "save" the Indians from being wiped out by teaching them to live as whites. The

Indians were asked to worship white men's gods, to work as farmers and cattle raisers instead of hunters, and to speak English. But the good intentions of these efforts couldn't mask the fact that to learn such things meant that Indians had to give up a way of life they loved.

Other white men doubted "savage" Indians could ever be civilized. These men simply wished to get rid of Indians—by killing them if necessary. All too often, the wishes of men such as these came true. It looked like the Cherokees had only two options: give up their lifestyles, or give up their lives. As he rode along the Cherokees' mountain trail in 1769, George Gist had no idea that one day a son of his would try to give the Cherokees a third choice.

After a few days of riding, Gist came to a village called Taskigi, on the Little Tennessee River. Taskigi was occupied by "friendly" Cherokees, and Gist knew from past experience that there would be no trouble.

Just outside the village, Gist passed by the communal farm fields of the Indians, where he saw the women tending green shoots of sprouting corn, beans, muskmelons, pumpkins, sweet potatoes, and tobacco. Beyond the fields was a prairie of green grass, rippling in the breeze. There women were roaming in the ankle-deep grass picking strawberries. Beyond that stood the forest, thick with all kinds of trees—oak, maple, pine, sourwood, hickory, as well as peach, wild apple, and plum.

Gist rode into town, followed by a pack of excited naked children, who ran after him, giggling and screaming. He passed by many small, boxy houses made of logs. The cabins were roofed in bark and shingles, with holes to allow the smoke from their fires to escape. He could smell venison roasting.

Gist rode to the center of the village and tied his horse next to the council house, where the chiefs of the town met to decide important issues. Some old Indian men who had been napping there on a bench joined the crowding children. Then the women ran from their homes, eager to see what new goods the trader had brought. There weren't many men present. They were still out on the hunt. "Good," thought Gist, "better to deal with women."

There was a hushed crowd around Gist when he opened his bulging packs. He displayed his first treasure, a mirror. It glinted

with the last strong rays of the falling sun as he turned it. The Indians admired it, passing it from hand to hand. Next he pulled out strings of brightly colored glass beads. The old men seemed most moved by these. One rubbed the beads against his wrinkled cheek and made a soft moan of approval.

The crowd responded with approval to each new treasure Gist pulled from his pack. He had iron kettles, pots, and skillets, which didn't crack as easily as the clay pots Indians made for cooking. He had shiny silver needles, red and blue wool strouding, sharp steel scissors, and many other useful items.

Gist stopped unpacking for a minute. He looked at the women, smiling and giggling as they hefted the heavy skillets or touched the sharp needles to their fingers. Then he saw her.

She was holding the small mirror he had passed out earlier. She was slim and graceful, with creamy dark skin and long shining black hair that hung to the middle of her back and was tied in braids. She held the mirror at eye level, staring in it as if she weren't sure who was looking back. She wrinkled her nose, then she closed one eye. She put a finger to her lips, to see if her image did the same. Gist watched her every move. She was lovely, he thought, a forest princess. For the moment he had forgotten all about furs and bags of silver.

Her name was Wu Teh, Gist learned later, and she was indeed special. She was from a very noble family of the Red Paint Clan, one of the seven clans of the Cherokee nation. She was the sister of three distinguished chiefs: Old Tassel, the wise peace chief; Doublehead, the fierce warrior; and Pumpkin Boy, the wily hunter.

Wu Teh was also charmed by Gist. She liked his broad shoulders, light complexion, his rugged, ready smile, and flint blue eyes. They talked only a little. She knew a few English words, and he knew no Cherokee. But they both understood Mobilian, which was a trading language made up of words from many Indian languages.

As Gist talked to Wu Teh, he saw more than just her lovely brown eyes and bright smile. He also saw an opportunity. Here

THIS LAND WAS MADE FOR YOU AND ME

was a chance to make a friend and gain the trust of these Indians. "I shall make a fortune," he thought.

After that day, Gist began to make regular trading trips into Cherokee country. With Wu Teh's help, he found it to be a very friendly place. On each trip, he sold all of his goods. He would stuff his empty packs full of beaver and muskrat skins the Indians paid him. In turn, he would sell the furs for huge sums of silver, for the skins were in demand everywhere, even in the great cities of Europe.

Every time Gist passed through Cherokee country, he would stop and visit Wu Teh. The other Indians saw that their beloved woman loved the white man, and so they accepted him. The number of skins they paid him for his goods became very generous, since he was a friend.

Soon Gist and Wu Teh grew very close. There was talk of marriage. The couple seemed very happy. Laughter could be heard from Wu Teh's little log house whenever Gist was in town.

But not everyone was happy about the coming alliance. Wu Teh's brothers, Doublehead and Pumpkin Boy, had helped raise Wu Teh when their father died. They were doubtful about the trader. They weren't very fond of white men as a rule, and this trader didn't seem to be an exception to that rule. They thought he was lazy, since he would only lie around while they and the other men were out on the hunt and Wu Teh worked in the fields. Then he would carry off all the skins they had caught. Something just didn't seem right.

Doublehead hated Europeans for many reasons, but there was one in particular. Before Gist had come to his village, many in his tribe had caught smallpox from white people. Some say that almost half of the Cherokee population was wiped out in just a few years by smallpox. Indeed, many more Indians were killed by the white people's diseases than by the white men's guns.

Not even the survivors of smallpox were spared. They were often left with large, ugly pockmarks on their faces and bodies. Doublehead was one of these survivors. But it had been so long since he had looked at his scarred face reflected in a pond that he had almost forgotten all about it.

One evening when Wu Teh and Gist were sitting by the fire in front of her cabin, Doublehead walked by. He saw the couple laughing together and his heart softened. Maybe this white man was different, he thought. Maybe he was a good mate for Wu Teh.

Doublehead walked up and greeted the couple. Wu Teh was busy admiring herself in her new mirror by the glow of the firelight. Doublehead gripped Gist's hand in friendship and smiled. Gist, who had begun to perspire nervously, breathed a sigh of relief. It seemed as if Doublehead would be his friend after all. This was a good sign, for in Cherokee households, a person's older brother had even more authority than a father. This is because the brother is related by blood to the mother's clan, which determines the family identity.

Doublehead saw the firelight glinting in Wu Teh's mirror. He picked up the mirror and looked at it. When he saw the ugly pockmarks on his face—the marks he had long forgotten—a terror seized him. He brought his hand to his face and began to rub, but naturally the pockmarks would not come off. He flung the mirror into the fire, shattering it against a rock.

"White men bring more than scissors and mirrors. They also bring death," Doublehead raged. He stormed away, leaving Gist sitting speechless.

After a brief courtship, Wu Teh married Gist, against the advice of Doublehead. The couple exchanged the traditional gifts at the simple wedding ceremony. She gave him a green ear of corn, and he gave her a fresh piece of venison. The corn symbolized farming—the woman's job. The venison was the product of the hunt—the duty of men. They each carried a blanket during the ceremony. They put both blankets together and each grabbed them at one end. Then the town chief pronounced "the blankets are joined," and the two were married. The couple moved to a new cabin outside the village, where they would not be bothered by Wu Teh's powerful and opinionated brothers.

As soon as the newlyweds moved in together, things seemed to change. Gist had never really loved Wu Teh. He had only used her to get closer to the other Indians. He wanted to get the best prices for his goods and feel secure among these "savages." Now that he was safely married, he had little time for his bride. He no longer listened patiently as she tried to find the right words to say. He always seemed to be busy counting and sorting his skins, and figuring out sums in his black ledger, where he recorded the amounts of silver he made. Worst of all, Gist began to drink. The more he drank, the meaner and more withdrawn he became.

Wu Teh was afraid to tell Doublehead what was happening, for fear that he would kill Gist. Instead, she went to see her third brother, Old Tassel, the wise, patient peace chief, who lived in the Cherokee capital of New Echota. Old Tassel counseled his sister to put Gist's things outside her door, which was the way Indian women divorced their husbands. Once this was done, the man had to leave, no questions asked, and the woman could take another husband. But Wu Teh hesitated. She liked this man when he was nice. She would wait and see.

Months passed, and though things got no worse, they got no better either. Then one night Gist was caught in the neighboring Cherokee village, selling whiskey to some young Indians. Selling whiskey in Indian towns was against the laws of both the Indians and the white men. But many traders did it anyway because whiskey brought a good price in skins.

Gist escaped from the chiefs who had caught him and galloped on his horse back to Taskigi. The men from the neighboring village were in hot pursuit. They were after his scalp. Gist reached Wu Teh's hut ahead of them. He quickly filled his packs, grabbed his ledger, and was off down the trail, never to be seen again.

When Doublehead heard what had happened, he was not surprised. His first impression of the trader had been enough. He was just like many other white men who had come before him, greedy for skins and silver. He didn't care what was good for the Indians, only what was good for himself.

When Doublehead reached Wu Teh's cabin, he found her alone in front of the fire, sobbing. He tried to comfort her. He didn't know that Wu Teh's sorrow was doubled. She was not only crying for a husband who was gone, but for a child who was on the way.

Wu Teh was pregnant, and her hot tears flowed as she thought of her poor, fatherless child.

3

The Old and the New

"Waaaa, hic. Waaaa, hic." The squall of a newborn baby broke the silence of the forest surrounding the little cabin.

Wu Teh cradled her new baby close. She tried to comfort him, although she wished she could cry too. She was lonely and sad to be a mother with no husband to share her pride in her new baby, a warrior, a son.

Wu Teh named him Sequoyah. She swore she would raise him as a Cherokee, though he was not a full-blood, as anyone could see from his light complexion, long nose, and thin lips. Wu Teh also gave the child a white man's name, George Gist, his father's name. This was often done when a child's father was a white man.

Wu Teh was more than just brokenhearted; she was ashamed. After Gist had fled, she heard about his other crimes, people he had cheated, and lies he had told. Wu Teh wished she had never met this white man, who had looked so kind and who had known so many things about the world beyond the great sea. How well he had hidden his evil ways! Wu Teh began to understand Doublehead's hatred of the white man. The white man was really two men. One was open, smiling, and good, offering help to the Cherokees. The other was hidden and evil, seeking only profit.

Sequoyah's exact birthdate is not known, but he is thought to have been born around 1770. He spent the first year of his life in a cradleboard, a small board with a deerskin pouch nailed to it. Sequoyah was fastened into the pouch, so that his whole body was covered, except his face and arms. Wu Teh strapped the board on her back and carried Sequoyah with her wherever she went.

When Wu Teh worked in the fields with the other women, she hung Sequoyah's cradleboard from the branch of a bush. Most of the other women did the same. Sometimes it looked as if a garden of little Indian babies had bloomed next to the fields.

If Sequoyah was cranky and cried, Wu Teh applied an old Cherokee remedy. She pinched Sequoyah's nostrils together, cutting off the air, until he gasped for breath. Cherokee mothers believed this treatment taught babies to cry only when they were wet or hungry, not just cranky. Mothers were too busy working to listen to impatient babies.

Wu Teh's small cabin was much like most Indian houses. Although three of her brothers were chiefs, she received no special treatment. The Cherokees, like most Indians, did not believe in any one person being much richer than all the rest.

As a child, Sequoyah's life centered about the fireplace inside the cabin. It was a mound of clay in the middle of the dirt floor of the house's main room. Sequoyah lay on the woven mats, warming himself by the fire and watching the orange flames lick the blackened iron pots of venison stew and corn porridge. He tilted his head back and stared out of the hole in the bark-shingled roof. He could watch wisps of black smoke from the fire reach out to the blue sky and disappear.

At night, when the cabin was dark except for the glow of the fire, Sequoyah would sit and listen to Wu Teh or one of his uncles tell stories. They told him about the sacred forest of plenty, where the spirits of good Indians go after they die. There they remained forever, hunting the spirits of animals killed on Earth. In this paradise, the Indians experienced all the feelings they knew on Earth. They could feel hunger and thirst, pleasure and pain. The only thing missing would be death. For bad Indians, there was the "other place." It was an evil place of pain, hunger, and darkness.

This place was located near the borders of the forest of plenty. The unfortunate souls there could hear the happy Indians rejoicing, but they could never share that joy.

The storytellers often reminded Sequoyah to take care of himself in this life, for his people believed that any injury received on

Earth would go with them even in death. Thus, if a person lost an eye on Earth, he would be one-eyed forever in the afterlife.

Old Tassel once told Sequoyah the story of an Indian who planned ahead for a good afterlife. When the man knew he was about to die, he shot his dog so that his pet could be with him in the spirit world. As Sequoyah listened to his uncle's tales, he stared at the deer and wild turkeys sewn in the tapestries on the wall. The flickering firelight made them seem to spring to life.

Although Sequoyah had no father, he had many adult companions. His uncles and other adults in the tribe often visited to play with him when he was growing up. In Indian society, adults generally considered all children as their own and treated them lovingly. An Indian chief once explained to a white man, "You English love only your own children. We love all children."

Sequoyah didn't miss his father, but sometimes he noticed a strange quiet come over his mother. At such times, she sat in the cabin and held the wool blanket Gist had given her when they met. Or she looked at the corner where he used to sleep, and her eyes filled with tears. She seldom spoke about Gist, but Sequoyah sensed that she was thinking about him.

* * *

In the morning Sequoyah was awakened early by the crowing of the rooster, the grunting of the hogs, or the lowing of the cows and sheep in the yard. The Cherokees had only recently begun to raise cattle like the white men did. They had always depended on wild game for their meat. They had laughed at the white man's habit of eating "lazy" cattle that were kept in a pen and lived only to be eaten. They preferred to eat an animal that had actually lived *to live*, whose flesh was healthy from running in the forest and eating what it found for itself.

But the presence of the white man was driving away much of the Indians' game. The white settlements, year after year, moved farther and farther into the Cherokees' woodland country, pushing the wild game farther and farther west. There were no more buffalo, and even deer were becoming hard to find. The Indians could no longer survive on meat they hunted, and they were forced to raise cattle too.

The Cherokees had little respect for the white people. When Sequoyah was allowed to sit by the fire with his uncles and the men, he listened as they smoked the pipe and told stories. He heard them joke about the way the skittish white man behaved in the forest, "like a spirit who merely floats there, and neither sees nor hears." But whether or not they liked the white people, the Indians' way of life was greatly affected by them.

The Indians' manner of dressing took on an obvious change. Very young children did not wear clothes, so Sequoyah and his playmates ran and played games about the village stark naked. Indian children may not have cared how they dressed—or if they dressed at all—but clothing style was a fairly important issue for the adults. They were greatly influenced by the white people's fashions.

It was not unusual to see an Indian man dressed the "New Way," in a cotton shirt with buttons, wool trousers, leather boots, and even a tophat. An Indian man dressed the "Old Way" wore buckskins and leggings and a feather in his hair. His face was streaked with paint. Often the Indians wore tattered castoffs from the white settlers. But to Indians who sought the New Way, even these old clothes were novelties and treasures.

The issue of the Old Way versus the New Way affected more than just clothing and cattle. Even Sequoyah, who was just a boy, understood that his elders often disagreed bitterly about which way was better.

The Cherokees had been known by the white people as a tribe of "friendlies." Their chief was called Little Carpenter, for his ability to build bridges of peace over even the most troubled waters. Little Carpenter liked the goods his people got from the white traders. He felt that white missionaries might be able to teach the

Indians many useful things. He had even traveled to England, where he met the "Great White Father," King George. Little Carpenter was very impressed with the grand city of London and with the king's hospitality. He vowed the Cherokees would be lifelong friends with the British, who controlled America.

But that was many years earlier. Now, in 1776, when Sequoyah was six years old, things were changing. England was losing control over its rebellious American colonies. Soon America would fight a war with England for its independence. The king could no longer offer the Cherokees much protection from the oncoming settlers who threatened to take the Indians' land. And Little Carpenter was more than ninety years old and senile. Many feared he was no longer capable of handling the affairs of the nation. He was letting his warm feelings for the White Father blind him to the fact that other white men were robbing the Cherokees.

One year earlier, in 1775, some white men persuaded Little Carpenter to sell off a huge piece of land. It was as big as the state of Kentucky and part of Tennessee. For all of that land, the chief had accepted a payment of a cabin full of rifles and ammunition, and some cans of red paint. The Cherokee who was most angered by this deal was a young war chief named Dragging Canoe, Little Carpenter's own son.

Like all Indian tribes, the Cherokees had many chiefs. Those whose council was sought in times of peace were called peace chiefs. Warriors whose advice was sought for combat were called war chiefs. Since the Cherokees had been at peace for a long time, their peace chief, Little Carpenter, had been their principal leader. But in recent years, as settlers pushed ever closer and violence between the Cherokees and the white men became more and more frequent, many began to feel the need for a new leader.

After Little Carpenter had foolishly sold the Kentucky land, Dragging Canoe had had enough. He defied his own father's leadership and called for all-out war on the white men. He had seen enough of their evil dealings.

For the past year Dragging Canoe had been raiding white settlements in Kentucky, trying to get back the land his aged father had practically given away. Dragging Canoe's raids were violent and bloody. He was trying to scare the white men off Cherokee lands forever. In fact, the Kentucky settlement got its name from Dragging Canoe, who called it *Gan Da Gi*, which in his language meant, "Dark and Bloody Ground." Settlers pronounced the phrase "Kentucky," and the name stuck.

Dragging Canoe could not persuade the majority of Cherokees to follow him in making war on the white men. Most of his people still followed his old father. But Dragging Canoe and his band were not alone in wanting war. Other inland Indian tribes to the north and south were also being pressured to give up their land. Many of them also felt a war with the settlers was inevitable.

In the spring of 1776, chiefs from several of these tribes met in council with the leaders of the Cherokees. They wished to unite the eastern tribes from the Great Lakes down to the mouth of the Mississippi River in a full-scale war against the white settlers.

Sequoyah was only six years old, too young to be a part of the council. But he sat outside the council house in New Echota on the evening the adults met with the visiting chiefs. Inside, the visitors sat crosslegged on the benches closest to the fire. In the middle of them was Cornstalk, war chief of the Shawnees to the northwest. He was dressed in buckskin covered in a flowing shawl. Around him were chiefs of many tribes—Chickasaws, Delawares, Ottawas, Senecas, and others. These tribes had been at war with the Cherokees in the past, but that was forgotten. All Indians felt threatened by a common enemy now.

Little Carpenter sat silently across from the visitors. His old, wrinkled face had two large scars on each cheek, and he wore a silver hoop in each pierced ear. The hoops were so large they almost touched his shoulders.

Wu Teh sat near the fire with her brothers, Old Tassel, Doublehead, and Pumpkin Boy, the three chiefs. Old Tassel's son,

Young Tassel the warrior, was also there, sitting one row behind his father. Sequoyah chose a spot outside on the grass to sit where he could see the fire and the people closest to it. He hoped the chiefs would speak loudly this night. He wanted to hear as well as see.

A group of men on horseback galloped up, raising a cloud of dust. At the head of them was Chief Dragging Canoe, dressed in buckskins, his face painted for war. The braves who rode with him also were dressed in the fashion of the Old Way.

Dragging Canoe and his men tied their horses and filed into the council house. Old Tassel and Doublehead greeted them with upraised palms. The chiefs then sat crosslegged on the front ring of benches by the fire.

The *adawehi*, or medicine man, opened the meeting. He wore a large wooden mask carved with a fearsome bird's face and carried a gourd rattle in his hand. He danced around the fire, kicking his legs out, shaking the rattle, and chanting a hymn to evil spirits, so they would not interfere with the council.

Cornstalk rose first to speak. He stretched out his arms with palms opened as if to embrace the entire gathering, and said, "My brothers and sisters, I have come to speak to you of the Old Way."

Cornstalk swung his arm in a wide arc over his head, tracing the path of the sun across the sky. This was the Indians' way to express the passage of time. "As the years have passed," he said, "the white settlers have stolen our land, and with it our way of life." Because the white people had run off the game, the Indians could no longer hunt. So they were forced to deal with the white traders, and to learn their language and ways. Soon, Cornstalk said, the white men would grow greedy for more land, until the Indians had none left and would be forced to roam in the wilderness.

Cornstalk said that the coming war between the English and their colonists gave the Indians a great chance. If all the Indian tribes, from the Great Lakes to the Gulf of Mexico, would unite, they could attack the white people from the west. Meanwhile the British would attack them from the east. Then the white people would be driven from their country forever.

Cornstalk raised his fist in the air. His eyes caught the glow of the firelight. "There is only one answer for our peoples, to rise up and drive the white men from our forests so that the wild creatures will return, and with them our old lives. We must return to the Old Way, and to do that, the white man must die."

4

"Take Hair and Horses!"

Cornstalk's speech whipped the council house crowd into a frenzy. Sequoyah peered in at the chiefs and men who talked heatedly among themselves, their flushed faces glowing in the firelight.

Cornstalk took the Shawnees' ceremonial war belts in his hands and approached Little Carpenter. At the old chief's side were the other elderly chiefs who supported him and wished to keep peace with the white men. Cornstalk offered Little Carpenter a war belt. The old chief sat rigid, his arms folded across his chest. He said nothing. Cornstalk offered the belts to the other old chiefs. They also ignored him.

Then, breaking the tense silence, Dragging Canoe bolted to the fire and shouted, "When the old sit silent, the young must act." Dragging Canoe walked right past his old father and took a war belt from Cornstalk's hand. Then Doublehead stood and did the same. Old Tassel winced when he saw his brother act so recklessly. But then Young Tassel, his own son, walked up and accepted a war belt too. Old Tassel was more hurt than shocked. He felt his family, as well as his people, were being torn in two.

Old Tassel knew someone must answer Cornstalk. He also knew that Little Carpenter would remain silent. The old chief was too proud to openly disagree with his hot-headed son, Dragging Canoe. But Old Tassel would speak, even though his son stood with a war belt draped across his shoulder too.

Old Tassel rose. He had only to lift his right hand slightly to hush the crowd. They had a great deal of respect for this wise peace chief, who had spoken well at so many assemblies in the past. Furthermore, they knew that after one speaker had his say, it was only right that another voice was heard. It was the Cherokee way.

Old Tassel began, like any good politician, by praising his opponent. "Cornstalk has spoken well. He is a brave war chief," Old Tassel said, bringing murmurs of approval from the crowd. "But the wisdom of wartime is folly in times of peace," Old Tassel continued. The crowd now turned edgy, sensing a fight.

"If we cut the skin of the white man, it is the Indian people who will bleed," Old Tassel said. He explained that making war with the white men would surely be a grave risk to the outnumbered Indians. Even if all the tribes united, there were still eight white men to each Indian. "Look at them! They are like the stars in the sky," he said.

"But even if we could take the hair of the white men to hang on our belts, we would feel the pain of the scalping knife," he said. Old Tassel listed all the goods that the Cherokees bought from the white men—the skillets, the mirrors, the steel scissors, and cotton and wool for making clothes. Then he looked out at the group and said, "Look at yourselves, brothers and sisters, before you condemn the New Way." They all looked at one another. Sure enough, most of them were wearing the shirts with buttons and the trousers of the white men.

Old Tassel named what they had learned from the white men. They had shown the Indians how to raise cattle, how to make clothing with the spinning wheel. White missionaries had opened schools to teach the Indian children about the Great Spirit, who made all people, Indians and white. Some children had been taught how to read and write with the books that contain knowledge on talking leaves.

Old Tassel hoped that the Cherokees could settle their differences peacefully with the white men. He agreed that it was wrong for the white settlers to steal Cherokee land. But King George had vowed to protect their land. Old Tassel advised that the Cherokees have patience and let the king and his redcoats deal with the settlers. In the coming war, the king would defeat the settlers, and keep his word to the Cherokees to guard their land. The Cherokees, meanwhile, must not take sides in the war. They could not afford to risk a fight when the numbers against them were so great.

Sequoyah smiled as he watched Old Tassel sit back down. He had often heard his uncle speak before, spinning tales in their cabin as the firelight burned low. But here was another Old Tassel, not a storyteller but a chief. Sequoyah felt his face flush with pride because he was related to such a man.

But the talking was not over. Dragging Canoe rose to speak now, and he seemed ready to explode. The muscles of his neck were tense, and his hands were balled in tight fists at his side. "The wise peace chief talks of things we have learned from the white man," Dragging Canoe began sarcastically. "He speaks the truth in this."

Dragging Canoe's raised voice seemed to reach out and grip each listener. Sequoyah felt his heart beat faster as the war chief ranted.

"We have *learned* not to be content with the good clay pots our mothers made for us. Now we crave the heavy iron skillets of the white man.

"We have *learned* to throw off our good buckskins, which are cool in summer and warm in winter, when the fur is turned toward the body.

"We have *learned* to favor the white man's wool flannel and cotton, which puts rashes on our skin and brings tears to our eyes. Yes, we have *learned* a great lesson from the white man."

Dragging Canoe paused and looked at Old Tassel. The crowd looked at him too. He was dressed in a shirt and trousers. Only the traditional turban and broach showed he was a Cherokee.

"You say that the white man has brought us many things," Dragging Canoe went on. "But he has taken away more. He has brought us his life, and taken away our own. We only raise cattle because the white man has driven away all our wild animals. Now he seeks to drive away our language and teach us his own. What need have we for another man's tongue, when we have our own. Do we need the white man to chew our food for us and stuff it into our beaks, like we are helpless baby sparrows?

"You say we must make peace with the white man. The white man does not know the meaning of peace. He has broken every treaty. He will never keep his word. Each year he asks for more and more land, and each time he says, 'This will be the last time.' Even now, after we have been cheated out of the *Gan Da Gi*, the white settlers move beyond it, into our land again. There will never be an end to the white man's greed until he has taken all our land. There can be no peace with people such as these. The only solution is their death. Death to the white men. Then we can return to the Old Way. We can wear buckskins, and hunt the wild game, and speak the tongue of our fathers and their fathers. This is our life. But to have it, we must bring death . . . death to the white men."

Before the stunned crowd could even react, Dragging Canoe motioned his braves to rise. Doublehead and Young Tassel went with them out of the council house. They mounted their horses and rode off.

Dragging Canoe sensed that the council would never vote to go to war with the white men. They would follow his father's policy of peace. That is why he left before the vote was taken. He was right too. The council voted against joining the visiting chiefs in their struggle.

Sequoyah thought about the council meeting on the ride back to Taskigi with Wu Teh. He had been very impressed by Dragging Canoe and his followers. Wu Teh and Old Tassel were angry at Doublehead and Young Tassel for joining the war chief. But Sequoyah couldn't help feeling a bit proud of them. He, too, had been moved by Dragging Canoe's speech. He had learned to love the Old Way as well, as he listened to the stories of Old Tassel and his mother. But as Old Tassel had often said, was it possible to expect the white men to disappear merely because the Cherokees want the Old Way? This didn't seem likely.

Perhaps the New Way was inevitable, Sequoyah thought. But did the New Way have to be the white man's way? Did the Indian always have to live on the chewed worms of the white man? Couldn't there be a different way?

For the next few weeks, nothing more was heard of Dragging Canoe, Doublehead, or Young Tassel in the village of Taskigi. But who could say what the fiery war chief and his loyal band of braves were likely to do?

Then, one day, a messenger ran into Taskigi and went directly to the council house. He spoke wildly to the chiefs gathered there. He was running from village to village to warn the Cherokees. Dragging Canoe had dug up the war hatchet. He had ridden north with his band of braves into the Kentucky territory. He went to the places where white settlers had blatantly cleared the forests and built cabins on Cherokee land. Dragging Canoe ordered his braves to "take hair and horses." They were to bring home as many white men's scalps and horses as they could find. Dragging Canoe's raiders took the scalps of women and children as well as men. He wished to scare the white settlers away, once and for all.

Old Tassel was in town visiting Wu Teh and Sequoyah. He shook his head slowly as he listened to the panting messenger. He knew the white people had come too far to be frightened away by such a small band of braves, no matter how fierce and determined they were. He knew what would come now, what *must* come.

The next day, and the days after that, Old Tassel kept watch in all directions, waiting for the signs. Then, one day, he saw them. He took Sequoyah to a high hill and pointed to the horizon in the north.

Sequoyah saw smoke in the sky where Old Tassel pointed. Big, billowing clouds of black smoke gathered above the treetops in the distance. They could have been mistaken for rain clouds, but they seemed to grow larger and larger. "They come," was all that Old Tassel said, placing his hand on Sequoyah's shoulder.

For the next couple of days Taskigi was a tense, watchful place. The clouds of smoke moved closer and closer. Then, early one morning, they came.

Sequoyah awoke to the sounds of women and children screaming, and the popping of rifles. He smelled smoke, and he knew the white men were in Taskigi.

Wu Teh suddenly grabbed Sequoyah by the arm and pulled him from his bed. She carried folded blankets, and Sequoyah could

31

see that she had wrapped pieces of cornbread and venison inside. Old Tassel was nowhere to be seen. Wu Teh hurriedly pushed Sequoyah to the doorway of the cabin.

Sequoyah peered out through half-closed eyes, hoping he was still asleep and dreaming all this. The town was a flurry of activity. Everyone was in a panic. Women and children were screaming and running in every direction. The hogs in their pens were squealing. Sequoyah heard rifle shots and saw a woman fall, her neck red with blood. Her little girl sat down next to her, bewildered. She touched her mother's wound and looked at the red stain on her fingers. Then another rifle cracked, and the little girl fell dead too.

Then Sequoyah saw the soldiers. They rode into the town in a cloud of dust, the dogs snapping at their horses. The soldiers fired their guns. They yipped and whooped and screeched the way Indian warriors did. They were mocking the Indians. There must have been hundreds of them. Sequoyah saw one of them ride up behind an old man and sink a hatchet into his skull. The old man fell in a clump and was trampled by another rider. Sequoyah felt his mother tug him to the back of the cabin. They pulled out some loose logs in the wall, crawled through the hole, and leaped into the woods under cover of the brush. Then Sequoyah and Wu Teh ran like deer from the guns of hunters.

Soon they came to the river. Beyond this was a thick forest that led to the base of the mountains, where they could lose themselves among the dense trees. But first they had to cross the river.

They heard the soldiers galloping up from behind. Sequoyah turned and saw black smoke rising above the town, and orange flames licking the black cloud from below. A group of soldiers rode into view, yipping and hollering wildly, still carrying torches.

The Cherokees from the village ran into the river and swam for their lives to the other shore. The ones with children had to go slowly and carry the little ones on their backs. Sequoyah could swim, so he and Wu Teh plunged through the water more quickly than some of the others.

Wu Teh and Sequoyah reached the bank. They crawled from the water, gasping for air, and ran for the cover of the brush. Sequoyah turned and saw the bobbing heads of his people still struggling through the deep water. The soldiers stood along the water's edge, firing their rifles into the river. Some of them smiled under their coonskin caps. Sequoyah saw men, women, children—his own playmates—stopped in the water by the whistling bullets, their faces frozen in a last look of surprise and pain. Then the bodies bobbed up and floated. Sequoyah looked at the river. It was flowing red with blood.

Wu Teh grabbed Sequoyah's hand and together they ran through the forest, stopping only to gulp a few mouthfuls of air into their stinging lungs. There were a few others who had escaped. They all ran and ran, deep into the forest, high into the hills, until they were out of danger. Then they gathered and made a hasty camp.

Wu Teh spread her blanket on the ground and lay the stunned Sequoyah down on it. Then she went to help tend to the wounded. Sequoyah looked around at the ragged camp. How many had died? Where would they go from here? Where was Old Tassel? Where were their men?

That evening the people of Taskigi huddled before a fire kept small so that the white men would not see it. All night the men from the village straggled into the camp.

The men had left Taskigi before sunrise that morning, in the hopes of surprising the white men before they reached the village. They never expected an army. There were more than 300 white soldiers on horseback, armed with rifles and torches. As the sun rose, the two dozen or so men attacked anyway, with a hail of arrows. But their bows and tomahawks were no match for the soldiers' rifles. Many Indians were killed, and the rest were forced to flee into the woods.

Still, they had not quit. They followed the army into the village, sniping at them with their arrows from the brush. They

33

would fight and flee, then fight again, in the way of the Indian. But this kind of warfare was useless against such a well-armed army of white men.

The soldiers put their torches to every house and shed in the town, and to the fields of crops. They burned everything to the ground. They shot every hog, slaughtered every cow, and cut the throat of every chicken. They even trampled the yelping dogs with their horses. The Indians, sniping and running in the woods, saw the carnage. They had to watch helplessly as their women and children fell dead and their houses collapsed in flames.

That night the survivors huddled around the tiny fire, nursing their wounds and crying for their dead. They were not sure who to blame for their sorrow. The white men had destroyed their village. But they couldn't help thinking that their real enemy was Dragging Canoe.

5 Secret Agent

The fair-skinned man pulled up on the reins of his horse, and the wagon creaked to a halt. The old wagon trail ended a little way ahead. After that, there were rocky slopes surrounded by a thick forest.

The hot noon sun beat down on his back. He had a load of rifles, shot, gunpowder, and whiskey. How was he going to carry it up this steep slope? The man mopped his sweaty brow. "Blimey," he moaned to himself. "I should never have left London."

The man bent down to pick up his canteen. As he lifted it to his parched lips, he suddenly noticed he was surrounded!

A dozen Indian braves were flanked around him, bows cocked, and arrows pointed at his heart. The braves were dressed in breachcloths and moccasins, with red war paint streaking their faces. Their heads were shaved but for a crest of hair down the middle.

The braves stared, waiting for a signal. The man made it, touching the index finger of his right hand to his pinky in a tipi sign. He was their man, their British secret agent.

One of the braves spoke, and Dragging Canoe stepped out of the forest and up to the wagon. He waved his hand, and the braves began unloading the wagon's cargo, disappearing with it into the woods.

Dragging Canoe's painted face wore no expression as he eyed the man. The agent took a small purse of silver coins from his jacket pocket and placed it in the hand of the war chief, who clapped it to his breast and stole silently into the woods.

"Well, not very talkative, that one," the agent chuckled to himself. "He could have had me up for steak and kidney pie."

The agent turned his wagon around and rode back down the grassy trail. He was glad this trip was over. He didn't like playing delivery boy for a band of Indians. But this was war, and one had to do many unpleasant things.

The British king had ordered his soldiers to put down the rebellion in the American colonies. The colonists had been demanding too much. No taxation without representation, indeed, fumed the king. He thought the colonists had other reasons for wanting to break away from England. They had presented him their scandalous Declaration of Independence this past July Fourth, 1776. But what they wanted was profits, not independence. They didn't want to pay the king any more of their trade profits. Well, he would see that they did. He had well-trained regiments of redcoats throughout the colonies, and reinforcements from Britain on the way. And the king had something else. He had a secret weapon to use against the colonists—the Indians.

The king used his agents in the colonies to keep in touch with bands of Indians who were unhappy with the settlers, many of whom were also rebellious colonists. Unhappy Indians weren't hard to find in America these days, especially in Cherokee country.

It didn't take long for the king's agents to make a deal with Dragging Canoe and his followers, who now included many disgruntled Indians from the Shawnee, Creek, Kickapoo, Choctaw, and Chickasaw tribes. The king promised to keep these Indians supplied with money, guns, and whiskey, if they would take care of some of his faithless colonists.

Dragging Canoe and his braves shouldered the cargo up the steep, rocky slope to their camp. Here in the thick mountain forests of southeastern Tennessee, in the shadow of Lookout Mountain, they were well hidden. Only an expert woodsman could find the way. Dragging Canoe had chosen a campsite near Chickamauga Creek, in the thickest part of the forest. It was the perfect place from which to conduct war.

The white militia that burned Taskigi had also leveled Dragging Canoe's Big Island Town in the Tennessee lowlands. But instead of rebuilding, Dragging Canoe relocated to this mountain hideout. He could fight and retreat, fight and retreat, for years from these mountains. Perhaps by then the British will have won the war, he thought, and the white men would at last leave the Indians in peace. At least, that is what he hoped would happen.

But what about the other Cherokees, the ones who wanted to keep the peace? Whether they liked it or not, Dragging Canoe was pushing them into this conflict too. He had gotten his way. The Cherokees were back in the forest, living the Old Way, hunting wild game for their meat and sleeping under the stars.

Besides Taskigi, dozens of other Cherokee towns had been burned down and hundreds of peaceful Cherokees had been killed by the white militia. More than 6,000 soldiers had been gathered from the colonies of Virginia, North Carolina, and South Carolina when Dragging Canoe's Chickamaugans started taking the scalps of white settlers. These angry settlers did not distinguish between the warring Indians and the peaceful ones who lived in the overhill towns to the north and west. And now some Indians were allied with the enemy, the British. The settlers would be even less likely

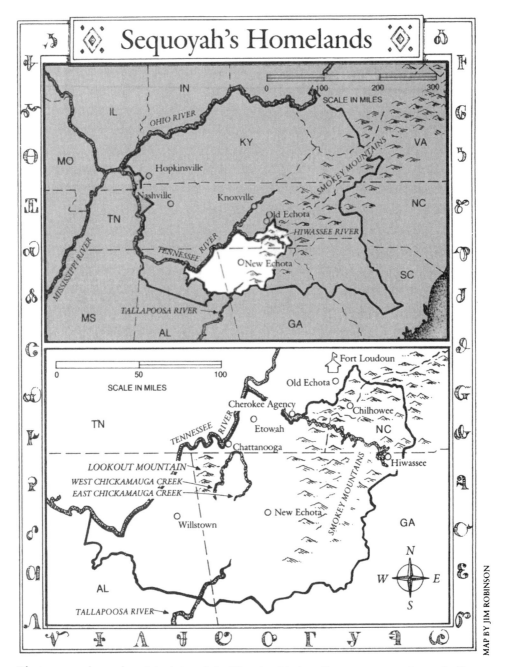

Sequoyah's Homelands

The top map shows the original size of the Cherokee Nation. Government treaties took all that land except what is shown in the small light area. The bottom map is a close-up of what was left.

MAP BY JIM ROBINSON

to try to determine if an Indian was hostile or friendly. They shot at all Indians now.

The people of Taskigi came out of the forests after weeks of hiding and scrounging nuts and berries to eat. They knew they were still in danger. As long as Dragging Canoe was fighting his own private war, all the Cherokees were in danger. Nevertheless, it was time to stop living like wild animals.

The people of Taskigi rebuilt their village. Men, women, and children pitched in to gather fallen trees to rebuild cabins and a council house. They planted new fields of crops so that life could go on as before.

Sequoyah did his share of the work, even though he was only a young boy. He found that he was quite a good craftsman. He worked easily with wood and tools, and he was helpful beyond his years to the men in the town. Soon he grew sturdy and very strong from all of his work.

At that time the federal government had signed treaties with all the chiefs guaranteeing the Indians protection from the settlers' militia. Whenever the Indians had problems, they were to bring them to the local Indian agent. While Taskigi and other Cherokee towns were being rebuilt, Old Tassel decided to visit the Indian agent to assure him the overhill towns had nothing to do with the Chickamaugans' raids. But Dragging Canoe kept raiding, and it was hard for anyone to stop the militia from taking revenge on all Indians. So Old Tassel again tried reasoning with Dragging Canoe.

One day Old Tassel rode to Chickamauga Creek with Sequoyah. When they arrived, Dragging Canoe folded back the flap of his tipi and the two chiefs held a meeting.

Sequoyah looked around the camp. There were several other braves milling about the settlement, most of them young and all of them dressed alike—in breechcloths and moccasins. The women tended the small patches of vegetables, or skinned the game, slicing and curing the meat.

The settlement itself was very crude. It was little more than a clearing in the trees, with a circle of tipis and a lean-to. But it was very beautiful, Sequoyah thought.

The Chickamaugans were warlike and irresponsible with the safety of the overhill Cherokees. Nevertheless, Sequoyah had to admit to himself that he liked the clean simplicity of their campsite. There was no smell of cattle manure, no cackling of chickens. The sound of the flowing creek washed over the camp constantly.

Sequoyah admired the Chickamaugans, but he also felt they lived in a dream world. How could they expect to regain the Old Way? The white people were here to stay. That seemed certain.

When the two chiefs finished talking, they came out of the tipi and stood in silence, their arms folded. The proud look on

Dragging Canoe's face told Sequoyah that Old Tassel's arguments had been in vain. The chiefs parted in peace. But they had only agreed to disagree.

Before Old Tassel and Sequoyah left the Chickamauga camp, they spotted Doublehead and Young Tassel, standing near a pit of ashes. On a pole nearby hung several hanks of hair, the scalps of white men. The warriors had celebrated with a scalp dance.

Doublehead stared at his brother with a puzzled look on his pockmarked face, as if he didn't know quite what to say. Behind him, Young Tassel stood, his normally bright and happy eyes cast down. He seemed ashamed to face his father. Old Tassel turned to the trail to leave. He would not interfere.

6

The Lessons of His People

Many a day Sequoyah woke to the sounds of distant rifles echoing along the ridge of the Smoky Mountains to the south. With the rebellious Americans fighting the British and the Chickamaugans fighting the Americans, he grew up surrounded by war. Sequoyah learned early that war was a fact of life in colonial America.

There were many less grim lessons to be learned in Sequoyah's world. But he didn't learn them in school. Schools were rare in Cherokee country at that time. Opportunities for learning were not, however, especially for a child like Sequoyah with a questioning mind. For such a person, every place he goes becomes a school.

Sequoyah had shown a talent for working with his hands when he helped the adults rebuild Taskigi. He also learned to help his mother stitch purple and white wampum beads, which the Indians used for money, into buckskin jackets or belts.

As Sequoyah grew older, he often wandered away from his mother's cabin to visit people and watch them work. One day, when Sequoyah was ten years old, he went to the cabin of Laughing Bear, the town's best woodworker.

Laughing Bear was an old man whose wrinkled skin was tough and leathery from spending so much time in the sun and wind. He was a strange, quiet man too. Day after day he sat cross-slegged in front of his cabin, wrapped in his weathered shawl, his long gray hair blowing, with a blank look in his eyes. But as Sequoyah watched the old man whittle, shave, and shape his wood, he believed what people said about Laughing Bear: "He hears the voice of the wood, and sees the faces hidden inside it."

Laughing Bear could make wood come to life. Whether it was soft pine or the toughest oak, he could create a work of art with his sharp blades and the sureness that still lived in his wrinkled hands.

Sequoyah went to watch Laughing Bear every day. For a while, he just sat in the circle of admirers who gathered around the old man. One day, Sequoyah brought his own piece of wood and the steel knife Old Tassel had given him. Laughing Bear peeked up slyly from his whittling from time to time to watch the boy's progress, careful not to let Sequoyah see him. After several weeks, when the old man was satisfied that Sequoyah truly wanted to learn, he decided it was time to speak to the boy. Laughing Bear seldom spoke to anyone. "You must look within the skin of the wood, to its soul," was all he said.

Sequoyah sat and carved with Laughing Bear week after week. He turned out pipes and bowls and figures of all kinds, and only the old man's occasional smile told him his work was progressing.

Finally, Sequoyah presented the old man with a gift he had been working on in secret. It was a pipe he had fashioned out of

43

hickory. He had soaked it in oil and rubbed it with sand to make the finish smooth and shiny. The pipe showed a duck grabbing a large trout with its feet. The tobacco was put into a bowl in the duck's tail, and the smoke was drawn through a hole in the fish's mouth.

Laughing Bear took the pipe and weighed its balance in his hand. Then he ran his wrinkled finger over the smooth finish. He was not smiling now, as he did whenever one of Sequoyah's works delighted him. His pleasure in the craftsmanship of Sequoyah's gift went deeper. His look was one of respect for what he saw. He took the pipe and wrapped it carefully in a piece of cloth, to show Sequoyah how much he valued it.

Sequoyah gradually stopped going to Laughing Bear and became an carver in his own right. By the time he was twelve years old, he had a reputation as a woodworker of great skill. He even began to get requests from people to make special things. He was once asked to make a stag's head pipe as a gift for a neighboring chief.

Sequoyah developed confidence as an artist. He began to think of himself as someone who was different from most Cherokees. He felt he was able to communicate with the spirits inside the wood, clay, stone, and other materials he used in his art. Trying to hear the spirit of an object is similar to paying attention to "intuition" or an "inner voice." It is simply finding inspiration.

Sequoyah sought out other members of his tribe with an interest in the spirit world. Among these were the medicine men. The Cherokees looked to their medicine men to interpret the spirit world. They believed that all things, people and plants, rivers and rocks, had spirits. Medicine men were those who discovered within themselves an ability to "hear" the messages of the spirits.

For the Cherokees, belief in various spirits was almost like a religion. The medicine men passed on the Cherokees' religion through stories of the spirit world and the world of mortals. Sequoyah became interested in these stories, since the spirit world was important to a budding artist. Hearing about it gave him inspiration.

The medicine men also knew other types of stories—historical stories, hunting stories, funny stories, sad stories. Storytelling was a big part of the lives of all Cherokees, and they depended on the medicine men to learn and remember all types of stories. It was the way they passed on their traditions and history from parent to child and grandchild. The storytellers were the "living books" of the Cherokees, and for most American Indian tribes.

To help them remember all of these tales, the medicine men used wampum beads. They arranged the beads to form pictures of main events in the stories. They stitched these pictures onto large belts, which were stored in a sacred place. These beadwork pictures didn't tell the whole story, just the main points in a tale. The storyteller would have to fill in the rest from memory. So the Cherokees' stories were seldom repeated the same way twice.

Sequoyah always tried to get a good seat by the fire when it was time for a story to be told. One of these occasions was the annual Green Corn Festival.

First there was dancing and the singing before the bonfire to celebrate the new crop of corn. Then the medicine man showed up, wrapped dramatically in a long blanket with a band of leather circling his wrinkled forehead. He sat down crosslegged before the fire, his worn face outlined by the bright blaze.

Sequoyah's eyes were riveted on the old man as he fingered the purple and white beads and talked and talked. The boy was amazed that such intricate tales could be held in the simple designs of the beads.

Sequoyah listened to the old man's deep, soothing voice. His eyes wandered from the man's bony fingers on the beads to the bright firelight, where he saw the story come to life. One night, the medicine man told the story of how hunting began in the world.

Once, a long, long time ago, shortly after the world was made, there lived on it only one small family, a man and a woman and their two boy children. In those early days, the world was lush, beautiful. It was inhabited by a spirit of harmony as never before. For not only the humans, but all of the beasts, and even the plants and trees and insects could talk to each other.

In those days, things came easily to humans. There were many edible plants and fruits, which were everywhere for the picking. And whenever the man went out to gather meat, he came home with game slung over his shoulder, so there was always plenty to eat.

One day, one of the two little boys became curious. He wondered where their father got the game that they ate every night. He never saw any animals running loose in the forest. He only saw what their father brought home for them to eat. One morning, he and his brother secretly followed their father when he went to fetch some game, to find out where he got it.

They followed their father up a winding trail through the hills until they came to a cave, whose entrance was covered by a small boulder. There the father stopped and rested. The boys hid themselves under some brush and watched. Then when he was rested, their father stood before the cave mouth. Holding his club in one hand, he moved the rock from the opening of the cave. As soon as he did so, a deer leaped out. Before the deer had gone far, the father sprang at it and clubbed it to death. Then he slung the deer over his shoulder, pushed the boulder back over the mouth of the cave, and went home.

The boys, who had seen everything, were very curious now and ran up to the mouth of the cave. They had to use a stick to pry away the heavy boulder that their father had moved so easily. Then they looked inside. To their amazement, the cave was absolutely filled with animals of every kind. There were deer and buffalo and wolves and beavers and raccoons and horses and opossums and squirrels and on and on. All the animals in the world were inside that cave, which was very large and reached back deep into the recesses of the mountain.

For a long time, the boys stood at the cave's opening, looking at the animals, many of which they had never seen before. Then they walked away to decide what they should do. But they forgot to put the boulder back. As soon as the animals saw the opening unguarded, they all sprang through it into the daylight until every last one had escaped from under the mountain.

And that is why humans now have to hunt animals for their food. Because those curious children were so careless.

When this story was finished, the medicine man cleared his throat and began another. Sequoyah watched the old man again finger his beads and begin the tale of how diseases began in the world.

A long time after the animals had escaped into the world, there were many more humans on Earth than before. Men hunted and killed the animals endlessly, until the beasts were afraid that they were in danger of being erased from the face of the earth. The animals met in a council before a great bonfire one evening to decide what to do. The bears spoke first. They said that since men hunted animals with bows and arrows, men should be hunted with bows and arrows by the animals. So the bears took it upon themselves to fashion bows from the strong hickory wood. One bear even sacrificed himself, so that good, strong bowstrings could be made from his entrails—which is how the Indians made their bowstrings too.

Once the arrows were whittled from some sturdy branches, the bears went to hunt men. However, when they tried to pull back their bowstrings, their claws hooked them, snapping them in two. The bears met again to discuss this problem. They wondered if they should clip their sharp claws in order to make war on the men. But they decided that this would be too great a sacrifice, since they would no longer be able to climb trees. So they gave up their plan to hunt the hunters.

All the animals met in council again. It was decided that they would fight the men in a more quiet, clever way. The deer had an idea. "Let's give men diseases," he said with a smile. The animals were in agreement immediately. Almost every animal had an idea for a disease, some horrible, some merely annoying. This explains why there are so many diseases that men can catch. The disease that the deer concocted is one of the most famous.

This deer, leader of all the deer, said that he would personally patrol the forests and watch the men as they hunted. If any man killed a deer without praying to the spirit of that deer for forgiveness, he would follow that man home, on the trail of blood left by the deer's bleeding carcass slung over the hunter's shoulder. Then, when he found the hunter, he would cause the man to have rheumatism, which would make him a cripple all of his days.

The animals laughed and laughed at their cleverness. But the trees and the plants, who were still friends of men, were listening. They decided to help the men. Each of them agreed to furnish a cure for one of the diseases that the animals had created, and to teach the cure to the men. This worked fine for awhile, until the plant kingdom forgot how to use the gift of speech. Then the plants could only tell the men of their powers by using their inner voices, the voices of their spirits. But only a few men were sensitive enough to hear the inner voices of plants and learn which diseases each could cure. These men became medicine men, and from that time forward they communicated with the plant kingdom to discover cures for all diseases.

Sequoyah always felt a little sad when the medicine man folded up his wampum belt and the fire slowly died. Sequoyah always wished for just one more tale. But that wouldn't have been enough. He would have wanted another, and another, even though his eyelids were heavy with sleep.

For days after he heard the medicine man's tales, Sequoyah repeated the stories to anyone who would listen. If his listeners were impatient little children, he often cut a little from his tale, to make it go more quickly. If they were adults, relaxing after a big dinner, Sequoyah told the tale slowly, adding bits and pieces from his imagination in places where it seemed best. He could often make his adult listeners laugh when he added new twists to stories they had heard so many times before.

Sequoyah grew to be as charming a storyteller as he was a talented woodworker. And he became quite popular. By the time he was a teenager, some of the men were eager to take him with them out on a hunting expedition. But Old Tassel insisted that the boy be prepared first. Stories and wit are good when sitting around the campfire, he said, but a man must know how to handle a bow and knife before he can be of any use on a long hunt.

Old Tassel left the cabin then, and Sequoyah sulked for a while, staring at the smooth dirt floor. Soon Old Tassel came back carrying something in a blanket. He unwrapped a hickory bow and a quiver full of arrows. "Here are your new tools, hunter," he said with a wink. "We shall see that you learn to use them well."

7

The Language of the Forest

Sequoyah raised the long blow-pipe to his lips and aimed at the squirrel twenty yards away. It had stopped to pick up an acorn in its forepaws and now stood gnawing it. Sequoyah filled his lungs with air, pursed his lips, and blew—puh!

The squirrel shivered. It flipped over on its back in the leaves and shook wildly. Then it stopped, dead.

The dart, tipped with snake poison, had acted quickly.

Sequoyah walked quietly toward his kill. The sun was just rising, and the sky had a dreamy glow. Sequoyah placed each foot carefully, trying not to make a sound.

He took the squirrel and stuffed it into his deerskin bag. He looked around. He didn't see any of the other hunters. They had blended into the forest.

This was Sequoyah's first hunting trip with the men of Taskigi. He was learning that to be a good shot with a bow or blowpipe was not everything. One also had to train the eye to take in every sight, the ear to take in every sound, and the mind to understand both. Every rustling bush, every thump and footfall, every twig cracking, was a word in the language of the forest. The words said: that rustling bush was a raccoon; that thump was a deer; that snapping twig was a hare on the run.

The first shafts of golden sunlight hung between the trees. Sequoyah stood and listened for a long time. The birds were all awake now and their chattering filled the forest. Sequoyah looked to his right and left. A tiny bird leaped from branch to branch. He saw nothing else. Not a creature stirred.

Suddenly, Sequoyah felt a hand on his shoulder. His eyes widened. He turned. It was Old Tassel!

Sequoyah had been listening intently, but he had not heard his uncle creep up from behind. Old Tassel pointed at spots in the woods around them where other Cherokee hunters crouched. Sequoyah had not seen or heard *them* either. How would he ever learn to move so stealthily?

Then Old Tassel pointed ahead to the prize all these hunters were inching toward. A deer, a big meaty buck, stood in the clearing about forty yards away. Its ears were pricked up. It had heard something and was ready to dash. Old Tassel motioned to Sequoyah not to move. The chief raised his loaded bow and aimed. In one motion, he pulled the string and let the arrow fly. It caught the buck square in its neck. Its legs gave out and it tumbled to the ground.

For several weeks, Old Tassel took Sequoyah out into a field and taught him how to aim and fire his new bow. He taught the boy to "see" and "feel" the target before he shot at it. He showed Sequoyah how to pick out a place on the animal's body and concentrate on it before letting his arrow fly. The arrow would do the rest. He also showed Sequoyah how to attract does by imitating the cry of a fawn, or by wearing false antlers made of branches.

Sequoyah went out often with the hunters. Each time he brought back more game. At first, he bagged a rabbit here and there and many wild turkeys. Then he began dropping his share of does. He began to feel at home in the forest, and his movements became as quiet and careful as a panther's. One day, he dropped his first big buck. After that he was accepted by the other braves as a hunter.

As the stack of pelts from Sequoyah's kills grew higher, Wu Teh gave him a lesson in trading. There were already many more skins than they would need for clothing or blankets. But the white men would pay dearly for them, if one bargained well.

For the first time in years, Wu Teh remembered the night that George Gist fled from her cabin, before Sequoyah was born. It was no longer a sad memory. She had long accepted the end of her marriage. Now she seemed to see something of her long lost husband in Sequoyah. Wu Teh would make a trader of Sequoyah, but she was also determined that Sequoyah would be a clever bargainer, not a cheater.

For years Wu Teh had advised people in Taskigi how to bargain with the white traders. She had learned a great deal from watching her swindling husband, who always thought she was so simple. She knew the traders' trick of giving the Indians cheap red paint and trinkets for their valuable pelts. Wu Teh taught Sequoyah to demand good silver for his skins, with which he could buy other goods. And she taught him the proper weight in silver he should receive for the different-sized pelts.

Soon Sequoyah made regular trips north to the trading post at Fort Loudoun. His packs were full of his pelts and his carved wood pieces. The traders at Fort Loudoun soon learned to respect Sequoyah. He could not be cheated, but he gave good value for the silver they paid him. And his wood carvings were of rare beauty and craftsmanship.

After a few visits, the word got out among the traders at Fort Loudoun that Sequoyah was the son of a white trader. Well, they thought, that explains his cleverness and talent. He isn't a full-blood "Injun." He's got some white man's blood. That's where his ingenuity comes from, they said to each other.

In an odd way, the traders were partly correct. Sequoyah had inherited something from his father, George Gist. It was the knowledge of how he and other white men had cheated Indians in the past. Wu Teh had told Sequoyah. Now he didn't fall for the white traders' old tricks. The traders called Sequoyah "clever." Indians who trusted white men, who could not believe white men would cheat them, were "stupid." To the white man, being clever meant not trusting people. Sequoyah's father had indeed inspired that lesson.

In order to deal with the traders at Fort Loudoun and other trading posts, Sequoyah had to learn Mobilian, a language spoken by all traders. Mobilian was a mixture of words from many languages, including Shawnee, Creek, Choctaw, Iroquois, and Chickasaw, as well as English, French, and Spanish. Using Mobilian, Sequoyah haggled and bargained in the marketplace.

Wu Teh thought Sequoyah's learning should go even further. She advised her son to enroll in the mission school in New Echota, where he could learn to read and write in English. She felt he would prosper much more quickly if he mastered the tongue of the white chiefs.

But Sequoyah scowled when Wu Teh suggested this. "I will not cut out my tongue," he snapped. "Nor will I eat the worms that the white man has chewed for me."

Wu Teh was distressed. She told her son that he was be ginning to sound like Dragging Canoe and her hard-headed brother, Doublehead. "Yes," thought Sequoyah, "maybe I am beginning to sound a little like them."

8

Forever Until Next Time

O ld Tassel stood before a large oak table that was covered by a map of the Cherokee nation. The United States government Indian agent, Mr. Pickens, ran his finger along a circular line drawn on the map.

"We will not cross this line in the future. Your lands will be safe forever," Mr. Pickens said.

Old Tassel said nothing. He thought of how many times the Cherokees had heard this promise in the past. In 1763 King George of England had drawn a line along the western border of the colonies, which, he declared, no white man would cross. The king had to redraw the line again and again because the settlers ignored it. But King George had no power anymore. Now it was the new American government that drew lines on the map and made promises to the Indians.

A lot had changed since the last lines were drawn. Little Carpenter was now dead and Old Tassel was the principal chief of the Cherokees. The Americans had beaten the British in their war for independence. The Cherokees had hoped the British would win because they weren't sure they could trust the land-hungry Americans. Now there was no choice.

Outside, a crowd of about sixty-five Cherokee chiefs listened quietly as Old Tassel explained the white man's latest treaty terms. "They will take no more land, forever," Old Tassel concluded. The chiefs were skeptical. They had heard such promises many times, but more than half of their land had been taken since 1763. Still they agreed to the treaty to avoid further war.

Pickens, standing at Old Tassel's side, surveyed the crowd of chiefs. "Dragging Canoe has not come," he said. "Will he make trouble?"

Old Tassel paused. Dragging Canoe had continued to raid, even after the white militia had burned out the Chickamauga settlements a few years before. The war chief simply moved farther south. But after the British left America, the Chickamaugans got no more supplies from them. Dragging Canoe was weakened, but he would probably never quit.

"If no white men enter our land, Dragging Canoe will have no scalps to take," Old Tassel replied. Pickens did not look satisfied, but he forced a smile and grasped Old Tassel's hand.

Later that day, Old Tassel and the other chiefs signed the Treaty of Hopewell. With it, the Cherokees placed the protection of their cherished lands in the hands of the young government of the United States.

Old Tassel had high hopes for this new treaty. He had worked hard to get it. He talked to all the chiefs. He tried to convince them that the only way to keep their lands was to cooperate with the white men. Dragging Canoe's ways would only lead to death. The chiefs had listened to Old Tassel and agreed to the treaty. Now as he rode back to New Echota, Old Tassel hoped that he had been right to trust the white men yet again.

As the new principal chief of the Cherokees, Old Tassel was a busy man these days. He seldom had time to visit Sequoyah and Wu Teh in Taskigi anymore. Sequoyah was becoming a man. He was almost fifteen years old now, and his training as a warrior was overdue. Old Tassel had wanted Sequoyah to wait for his training

until the war between the British and the colonists was over. The chief had felt strongly that the Cherokees had to remain neutral in this fight. But now that the war was over and peace seemed secure, Old Tassel couldn't see any reason at all for his nephew to train as a warrior.

Wu Teh had begun to recognize Sequoyah as the man of the house. Before, she had waited until Old Tassel visited to make any important family decisions. But Sequoyah had become a good hunter and provider, as well as a talented artisan. And he was a clever trader, whose good humor made him welcome wherever he went. He was, indeed, a son to be proud of.

One day, Sequoyah went out hunting with two of his friends, Rabbit Eyes and Agi Li, a half-white boy. Both of Sequoyah's companions wore used trousers and shirts which they had bought from the white settlements. Sequoyah, on the other hand, wore buckskins and the traditional Cherokee turban wound round his head. Just as he would not speak the white people's language, he would not wear their clothes. He never tried to argue with his friends about their preferences, however. He preferred to let people be what they would be.

In the forest that day, the three young hunters picked up the trail of a deer. They followed its hoofprints in the dirt and leaves for hours, hoping it would lead them to the whole herd. Then each of them might bag a kill.

After several hours of stealing silently through the forest following the deer tracks, the boys crept to the crest of a hill. In a meadow below, by a small brook, were the deer. The boys smiled at each other. They were thinking how proud the men would be when they returned, each with his own deer. The boys carefully raised their bows and waited for the moment to shoot. Then, faster than a thought, one of the deers shuddered. The whole herd leaped into a run and in seconds were lost among the trees.

Sequoyah and his friends looked at each other in bewilderment. How had they scared the deer away? Then they heard a group of white hunters coming from the forest behind them, laughing and singing loudly. The men had scared the deer away.

The boys turned to see three bearded men carrying muskets on their shoulders and leading a horse with a deer carcass slung across its saddle. The men approached the boys, smiling and offering handshakes to their fellow hunters. These white men were loud, but they seemed harmless.

The group built a fire and made some coffee, which the white men had brought. They wanted to compare hunting strategies. One of the white men knew some Cherokee, so he acted as interpreter. Using gestures and their few words of English, the boys explained that they had been tracking deer when the white men came and scared the animals away. The white hunters were genuinely sorry. They knew how clumsy they were in the forest compared to the Indians. But frightening off the deer had been an accident. Finally, everyone ended up having a good laugh over the incident.

As the two groups talked, the sky darkened. A storm was coming up, and they had no shelter. Quickly, the three boys tied the tops of some small trees together in an arch and made a roof over them with brush and bark. In a few minutes, they had completed a shelter big enough for all of them, just in time to keep out the rain that began to pour down.

It rained hard for a long time. The group sat under the shelter, where they had a warm fire and plenty of dry wood.

Rabbit Eyes and Agi Li napped for a while, but Sequoyah remained awake. He listened as one of the hunters read aloud to his friends from a leather-bound book. On the cover of the book was written the title and author: *Gargantua* by François Rabelais.

As the man read, his two companions broke into laughter from time to time. Sometimes they just chuckled. Other times they cackled and seemed ready to collapse with hilarity. The reading and laughter reminded Sequoyah of the times when he heard the medicine men tell stories. These tales often made him laugh. "That book," he thought, "must be like the wampum beads of the medicine men."

When the reader stopped to rest his eyes, he tried to explain to Sequoyah what was so funny. Sequoyah understood now that the story was about a giant man who did many peculiar things, such as drinking milk straight from the cow. Sequoyah thought many of the jokes were stupid, but he was amazed that the small book could contain such a long tale.

Sequoyah picked up the book to examine it. He saw that it was made of thin leaves of paper. Instead of the pictures on a wampum belt, there were marks of some kind on the paper, like the footprints of a crow. And the marks were in neat rows like the rows of corn planted in a garden. When the reader looked at these rows, the leaves of the book "talked" to him. The reader then told his friends what the leaves said. Sequoyah found these talking leaves fascinating.

Sequoyah mentally compared the markings on the talking leaves to the designs on a wampum belt. The colorful belt was much prettier, but the book was filled with many thin leaves, each covered with markings. It must surely "remember" more than the wampum belt. Wu Teh had told Sequoyah that books made the white people's medicine powerful. She had said that just one of their books of talking leaves could remember more than all the medicine men of Taskigi together. And the white men had many, many such books. This was why Wu Teh wanted Sequoyah to learn English—so he could learn the secret of the talking leaves, the secret of the white people's powerful medicine.

Sequoyah was so curious about the talking leaves that he bought the book from the hunter for two good deer pelts. The men laughed, thinking they had again cheated an Indian. Sequoyah knew his pelts were worth more in silver than this book. Still he wished to have it. He wanted to ponder the secret of its talking leaves.

Agi Li and Rabbit Eyes kidded Sequoyah as the three hiked home after the rain stopped. "You gave good pelts for a book you cannot even understand," they said, laughing.

Later the boys fell to talking about the talking leaves. "Surely," Rabbit Eyes said, "it was a magic power of the white man to be able to put his speeches into books."

"Surely," Agi Li said, "one must learn the white man's language to gain the power of the talking leaves."

Sequoyah bristled at this. "Bah," he said. "These are mere scratchings, mere crow's prints. It is not magic. I could invent them for the Cherokee language, and we, too, could have our own talking leaves."

The other boys laughed at this. "How can you do such a thing?" asked Agi Li, chuckling.

Sequoyah picked up a flat stone and scratched out a picture of a deer on it with the blade of his knife. "There," he said, showing them the stone. "That means 'deer,' see?" Then Sequoyah drew an arrow through the deer. "And that means 'to hunt a deer,'" he said.

His friends laughed again. "At this rate, you will be scratching on stones until you are an old man, Sequoyah, to make pictures of every word there is in our language. It is impossible. The talking leaves belong to the white man. They are not meant for us."

Sequoyah stood his ground. "You are wrong," he said. "You think the white man has special medicine. That is why you wear his clothes," Sequoyah said, pointing to their trousers and shirts. "Well, our medicine can be just as strong, if we wish it."

9
The Lame One

Sequoyah sat and looked at the book by the light of the fire. For a long time he turned the pages and scanned the rows and rows of marks he could not understand.

"If the Cherokees had talking leaves such as these," Sequoyah thought, "they would not have to wait for special occasions to hear stories from the medicine men. They could have them whenever they chose—even at home, sitting alone by the fire."

Sequoyah looked at his hands, then at the many beautiful wood figures he had carved with them. "I can make anything," he said to himself. "Surely I can draw talk."

He began to make pictures with a stick in the smooth dirt floor near the fire. He drew the deer's head again, with an arrow in it. But this time the picture seemed to mean "hurt" rather than "hunt."

He scratched other pictures in the dirt. After an hour he grew tired and his mind became confused. He looked down at the symbols he had made. He had crossed out half of them because they were unclear. And he had forgotten what most of the others were supposed to mean. If he worked this long with his knife and a piece of wood, he'd have something to show for it now: a carved face or animal. But this drawing of talk was a different kind of problem. It made him dizzy to think about it.

Sequoyah took the book he had bought from the hunter, wrapped it in a piece of cloth, and put it away on a shelf. Then he lay down to sleep.

As Sequoyah lay there, he thought that perhaps his friends were right. Maybe the talking leaves were meant only for the white people, and if Cherokees wished to share their magic, they would have to learn the white man's tongue.

As Sequoyah drifted off to sleep, the story told to all Cherokee children flashed across his mind.

> *In the beginning, the Great Spirit gave all peoples gifts. He gave the book to the Indian, and a bow and arrow to the white man. When the Indian was asleep, the white man stole the book from his hands and left the bow and arrow. Then the white man learned how to read the book, and the Indian learned to live by the bow. Now the book belongs forever to the white man and the bow belongs to the Indian.*

Sequoyah dreamed that the white hunter who sold him the book entered his cabin. The man took the book from the shelf, saying angrily, "This is not meant for you." Sequoyah woke with a start. He jumped up and went to the shelf. The book was still there. He unwrapped the cloth anyway, just to make sure. There was the book, with its scuffed leather cover. Sequoyah held it in his hands for a few seconds, then he said, "Bah! That old story of the book. It is a fable for children." He wrapped up the book in the cloth, put it away, and went back to sleep.

64

Sequoyah didn't think about the book again for a long time. His life was full and he was a busy young man. He spent his days hunting or traveling to the trading posts around Taskigi. Often other men would ask him to trade their pelts for them, since he got such good deals. Sequoyah was happy to do this and he never asked for a commission. Nevertheless, many of the men insisted on paying him one.

And so Sequoyah prospered. Little by little, the cabin filled up with things he acquired for trade. Soon he had a loom, a sewing table with a stool, two rocking chairs, a butter churner, carpets and blankets, rifles, pistols, powder and shot, shirts and several pairs of pants, candles, jars, and various pots and pans.

Though Sequoyah prospered, he still kept the Old Ways. Most mornings he would rise before the sun and go hunting with the other men. The more time he spent with them, the more impatient he grew to become a warrior. Every Cherokee boy waited for this time. To become a warrior was to become a man. Sequoyah knew that Old Tassel frowned on the idea. The old man felt that warriors weren't needed if peace was maintained with the white man. Sequoyah hoped that one day he could convince his uncle to change his mind.

One evening during a long hunt in the western lands, Sequoyah sat by the fire with some of the men. The fire was dying down to a reddish glow, but the stars were bright and the hunters were restless. A brave began to talk about the trials of becoming a warrior. He spoke in an eerie voice, as if he were telling a ghost story. He knew Sequoyah and his young friends would be listening. He talked about the long days of fasting and the tests of endurance. The other braves who had been through the trial before chuckled at each horror he mentioned. They knew that the storyteller was trying to scare the boys. Sequoyah knew it too. But he couldn't help feeling weak and feverish. What was wrong? He usually felt strong and eager when he heard of a challenge. Did this mean he was a coward?

When Sequoyah returned home from the hunt, he had chills. He wrapped himself in blankets and lay down to sleep. When Wu Teh came in she found her son huddled in front of the fire, his

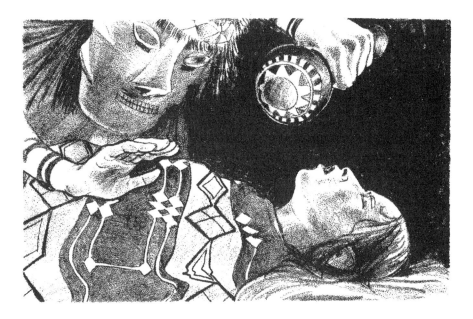

brow covered in sweat. She touched his face. It was hot with fever. She put a damp cloth on her son's forehead. Then she went to fetch the medicine man.

In a few hours, the entire cabin was transformed into a center of Cherokee medicine. The medicine man put on a frightful mask with a broken nose to scare away evil spirits. He circled Sequoyah as the boy slept, shaking his gourd rattle and chanting a low, mournful song.

Wu Teh sat by the fire. Next to her was Ali Gee, Old Tassel's wife, and a woman who worked for her. These three would watch Sequoyah night and day until he felt better. As the women waited, they kept a lookout for signs of a witch entering the cabin. The Cherokees always did this when someone was ill. They believed that witches could sap the last bit of strength from those too weak to protect themselves, killing them. This was how witches survived.

Hanging above the fire was a large, black, iron cauldron. It was filled with river water and some roots and plants that the medicine man brought. As the pot began to boil, Wu Teh stood up and went to stir the bubbling broth. The medicine man chanted softly. When he finished, he moved over to the fire and lifted the pot, setting it aside. He took a pinch of dried tobacco in his hand. The women came forward nervously.

The medicine man let the tobacco float down into the center of the fire. If it caught fire in the air, it would float in a certain direction, which would show everyone where to watch for witches. If the tobacco ignited in a sudden "pop," it meant that a witch was already in the room. The tobacco floated down into the fire and burned quietly. The women sat back and sighed in relief.

The medicine man held up Sequoyah's head and put a cup of warm broth from the pot to the boy's lips. Sequoyah drank down the brackish, black broth in one horrible gulp. In seconds, he put his face into a bucket at his bedside and vomited. This is just what the medicine man had intended to happen. He wanted to empty the boy of all evil influences.

Wu Teh wrapped Sequoyah in blankets. The women carried him next door to the sweathouse, a small, cone-shaped hut made of bent boughs lashed together and covered with rushes and blankets. They laid Sequoyah down on soft quilts. Outside the sweathouse, rocks had been heating in the fire. The women rolled them into the hut with sticks. Then they poured water over the hot rocks to make thick clouds of steam and closed the doorway of the sweathouse. Soon the hut became hot and muggy inside, and Sequoyah was sweating from head to toe.

After a while, the women helped Sequoyah to his feet. The damp blankets clung to his skin. His hair, usually covered by a turban, was wet and pasted to his scalp. His eyes had a vacant stare. Wu Teh lifted her son's arm around her shoulder and helped him walk down to the river.

At the river's edge, Wu Teh took Sequoyah's blanket and he dove naked into the icy cold water. He swam weakly for a few seconds; then his head bobbed up. His lips were blue and trembling. The medicine man looked on approvingly, saying nothing.

These treatments were standard Cherokee medicine, but they didn't seem to do any good. Nothing seemed to work. These chills and fever were not the sign of a coward, as Sequoyah had thought. They were the symptoms of a serious disease that would change his life.

After two weeks, Sequoyah's fever finally broke. His face bloomed with rosy color again. He felt much better except for one thing. When he got up to stand, the muscles of his left leg seemed to be made of water and would not hold him up. And his leg throbbed with pain each time he put his weight on it.

After a while, Sequoyah could stand and even hobble around without any pain. But the leg was still not strong. He could not walk evenly as before. He dragged his left leg behind him.

The story went around that Sequoyah had had a hunting "accident," since he took ill shortly after returning from a hunt. People assumed that he had forgotten to ask forgiveness from the deer he had killed and that the Little Deer had followed him home and given him rheumatism. More likely, Sequoyah's "accident" was a bout with the crippling disease polio. In that case, he was lucky to come out of it with only one lame leg. In those days, the disease often left people completely crippled. There were no vaccines.

Whatever his disease had been, Sequoyah was suddenly handicapped. His young life changed. He was barely a teenager and had wanted to train as a warrior. Now that seemed impossible. How could he run after an enemy? He could no longer even keep up with the rest of the hunters. He didn't want to slow down the hunt, so he stayed at home. He could still ride his horse to Fort Loudoun, but he felt awkward hobbling about in front of white men. They always snickered as he limped past, and he knew they were making fun of the "crippled Injun." Even his own people stared when he limped, dragging his lame leg. Sequoyah began to spend a lot of time in his cabin, to avoid the embarrassment of trying to walk.

He sat in the cabin and stared into the fire, hour after hour. He began to worry, wondering what on earth to do. "What if my leg never heals," he said to himself. "Then I shall go to my death a cripple, and I shall live the life of a cripple forever in the hereafter. I shall limp for eternity!"

Sequoyah tried to buck up, but, with nothing to do, he dwelled on his illness. He needed a project. He had always been constructive. He had to get busy. Then he remembered the book wrapped in cloth on the shelf.

Sequoyah unwrapped the book and again pondered the problem of how to write down the talk of the Cherokees. He gathered strips of bark, and began to make pictures of words on them with his knife. It felt good to be working with his knife and a piece of wood again. This challenge excited him.

As he cut into the wood with the sharp blade, his confidence swelled. "What is there to this? I have made many things before out of wood," Sequoyah told himself. "I can make talk out of wood, too."

Sequoyah thought about the story of how the white man stole the book from the Cherokees and gave them the bow and arrow. "Foolishness," he thought. He reasoned with himself while he carved picture after picture into the bark. The Cherokees did not have talking leaves only because no one had made them yet.

Sequoyah began to think that the white men's talking leaves were like a house for the words of their language. The Cherokees' language had always lived free, in the speech of the people. Sequoyah would build a house for their language, so that the words could be kept in one place.

Sequoyah worked with a deep sense that he was doing something very necessary. He had heard, from his mother and his friends, that talking leaves were what made the white man's medicine so much more powerful than that of the Cherokees. It was what helped the white men to make knives of shining steel, and

guns that shot great distances. It let them create the far-seeing tubes they called "telescopes." With this tube one could watch a man smile across a wide river.

The Cherokee culture was basically the same when Sequoyah was born as it had been for hundreds of years before. There had been little change in their way of life. On the other hand, the white Europeans' way of life had changed continuously, aided by their expanding store of written information. Their new inventions helped them discover the seas and conquer other nations.

Sequoyah wanted the power of the talking leaves for his people. If the Cherokees accepted the white man's talking leaves, the New Way would always be the white man's way. If they could write their own language, perhaps the Cherokees would have their own New Way.

Make Him Dreadful

O ld Tassel and a few other chiefs rode slowly along the trail outside the town of Chilhowee. They were looking for the camp of the white militia, who were under strict orders to kill Old Tassel.

The United States government had not been able to keep the white settlers in Kentucky within the boundaries drawn by the Treaty of Hopewell. When the settlers again moved onto Cherokee lands, Old Tassel had chosen not to drive them off, even though the treaty gave him that right. He preferred to wait until the United States government could find a way to relocate the settlers.

But Dragging Canoe had not been patient. He had led his warriors in new raids on the settlers, scalping them and burning their settlements. When some settlers escaped his tomahawk, he and his braves chased them back into white territory and killed them there. That had angered the white settlers and their militia. They blamed Old Tassel, the Cherokees' chief, for these deaths.

Old Tassel sent a messenger to the head of the militia. "They are not my people who spilled the blood and spoiled the good talks. My town is not so; my people will use you well whenever they see you," Old Tassel said. But the white officials would not listen. They still wanted his blood.

The soldiers stormed into Cherokee territory in search of Old Tassel. On their way, they sacked and burned the town of Hiwassee. After the attack, Old Tassel sent another messenger to the militia. He still wished to meet with their captain and try to find a way to make peace. The militia captain agreed to a meeting.

Old Tassel was accompanied to the meeting site by Chief Hanging Maw and two other Cherokee chiefs. Old Tassel rode down the trail at the head of the line, carrying a white truce flag.

At a bend in the trail, Old Tassel and the others saw smoke above the treetops. They rode on, right into the militia's camp. Old Tassel raised the white flag, and the others held both hands high to show they were unarmed. The soldiers were sitting about the camp eating as the chiefs rode past them.

The Indians came to a halt before the commander's tent, where another white flag was flying. "We come in peace," Old Tassel said loudly. The commander stepped out of his tent. He was not in uniform, and was unarmed. "Greetings, Old Tassel. We have much to discuss," he said.

The rest happened quickly. A soldier who had been watching quietly grabbed his musket. He rose and shouted, "Death to the murderous savages!" Then he shot Old Tassel in the head and the other soldiers began to fire. The shooting was over in seconds. The bewildered commander ran to Old Tassel, who lay slumped over the front of his horse. The Cherokees' chief was dead. The other chiefs lay dead on the ground.

Sequoyah heard the rider come shrieking into town. He wrapped his book and pieces of bark in the cloth and put them on the shelf. He didn't pick them up again for many years. What had happened changed everything for a while.

"Old Tassel has been murdered by the white men," the rider shouted from the front of the council house. "Murdered, with the white flag of peace in his hand."

The Cherokees were paralyzed with grief. But for Wu Teh and Sequoyah, it was a double tragedy. They had lost more than a chief. They had lost their beloved brother and uncle.

There was a great crowd present at Old Tassel's funeral. Young Tassel was sorrowful but he stood proud and defiant as the medicine man chanted the hymn to the spirits of the dead. Dragging Canoe himself was present. Even he was sad. He had disagreed with the old chief, as he had with his own father. Nevertheless, Dragging Canoe knew that Old Tassel had acted with honor and done what he thought was good for his people.

Doublehead's face showed no expression. He had sworn to avenge his brother's death, but now he stood silently beside Sequoyah and Wu Teh. They all listened to the medicine man beseech the spirits of the dead to welcome their old chief among them.

Meanwhile, many white men were growing nervous. The militia leaders claimed that there had been no orders to kill Old Tassel, that a soldier had done it on his own. The Cherokees didn't believe them.

Sequoyah no longer had much sympathy for white people. If they could kill Old Tassel, a man who sought nothing but peace, then Dragging Canoe must be right about them after all. These white men were not to be trusted. They had to be destroyed. Many other Cherokees felt the same.

The militia had killed Indians merely because they were Indians, without bothering to determine who were friendly and who were not. The Cherokees, in turn, began to hate all white people merely because they were white.

Most of the Cherokees had long supported Old Tassel's peace efforts. Now they began to see things as Dragging Canoe did. They began to believe that the only way to deal with white people was with the bow and tomahawk.

The Cherokees moved their capital from New Echota to Ustanali in Georgia, near Dragging Canoe's village. They wanted to be under Dragging Canoe's protective wing and to support the renegade Chickamaugans. Old Tassel would have been surprised to see how quickly his death had united his people. This unity was something he strived for but could not achieve in his lifetime.

Sequoyah painted bright red streaks on his face. He would make his body hard. He would become a warrior. He exercised his lame leg day after day. When he ran he put as much weight on his leg as he could without falling. Despite his efforts, he fell often. Wu Teh grieved for her son, but she saw no way to comfort him. When Sequoyah got an idea fixed in his head, it stayed there. He would be a warrior, lame or not.

Sequoyah sent messengers to Doublehead at Nickajack, one of the Chickamaugans' new strongholds. He pleaded with his uncle to be his sponsor in becoming a warrior—to "make him dreadful," as the Cherokees said. But since Old Tassel's murder, Doublehead had been very busy, raiding and adding scalps to his belt. He ignored the messages.

One day, however, as Doublehead was riding through town, he saw Sequoyah running and exercising his weak leg. The boy's painted face was dripping sweat. Sequoyah had the look of someone who was possessed by spirits. Even Doublehead was moved.

Finally, Doublehead agreed to sponsor Sequoyah. Soon all was ready. The night before the ceremony, Sequoyah drank the foul-tasting "black drink" that made him vomit. Cherokee men used this drink to help purify their bodies before many occasions, both solemn and recreational. A Cherokee man might purge himself before a council meeting, a battle, or even a game. The cleansing was believed to bring the body's powers to a peak.

The next morning, Sequoyah stood naked on a high hilltop. The medicine man gave the ceremonial chant, asking the spirits to make Sequoyah brave. Then Doublehead took the bone of a wolf

that had three sharp points and raked it across Sequoyah's body. As Sequoyah stood with his arms out-stretched, Doublehead drew the sharp bone across Sequoyah's back from one wrist to the other, then down the length of his body. The bone drew blood as it cut into his flesh. As his body was being torn, Sequoyah stood absolutely still. Not even his lips quivered.

When this raking was over, Sequoyah's whole body was bloody. He ran, limping, to the stream and dove into the icy water to purify himself. When he came out of the water, he was washed with a steaming broth of herbs and roots mixed by the medicine man.

After this was over and Sequoyah had been purged, stripped, raked, bled, chilled, steamed, and washed, he stood before Doublehead. He felt like an empty bottle. Doublehead looked in Sequoyah's eyes and said, simply, "Go."

Sequoyah knew what this meant. For the next seven days and nights, he was to leave the town and live alone in the hills.

Sequoyah went south to the high hills. For seven days and nights he lived on nuts, berries, and fruit while he contemplated the warrior's life. If he began to think about giving up, he turned his thoughts to Old Tassel's murder. If he thought about returning to his warm cabin to rub bear fat on his stinging wounds, or to soak his throbbing leg in hot water, he remembered his uncle. His body was tempted but his will was strong, bent on revenge.

On the eighth day, Sequoyah returned. Doublehead delivered an address to the Great Spirit, welcoming another warrior into the fold. Then he placed a steaming dish of partridges and mush before his hungry nephew. To the Cherokees, the partridge's loud flapping of its wings represented thunder, and its quietness while sitting or walking signified stealth and cunning. The power of thunder and the wisdom of cunning were what the Cherokees valued most in a warrior.

11
Man Killer

The braves were hidden in the forest near an orchard where there were rows of trees loaded with ripe red apples. The Indians were just outside the ghost town of Setico. A small band of the white militia was riding toward the deserted town. The Cherokees hoped the soldiers would find the apples tempting. They watched and waited, as quiet as the trees.

Sequoyah felt his stomach rumble as he looked at the apples. He had fasted the previous day, which was the custom for the first day on the warpath. Today he had eaten only one handful of cornmeal, the limit for a warrior. But he was hungry for more than food today. He wanted revenge.

The leader of the raid made the crow's call, "Kaaaw, kaaaw." This signal let the braves know that the *Unakas*, or white men, were approaching. Dozens of

Cherokees peered silently from the trees as the soldiers rode across the stream and up the hill into Setico.

The white men tied their horses and explored the town, thinking it was deserted. One man found the orchard and let out a shout, "Hey, ripe fruit! Come and get it." The Cherokees gripped their tomahawks tighter.

The men climbed up the trees, laughing and picking the ripe fruit, just as the Cherokees had hoped. Sequoyah saw that the soldiers carelessly left their rifles leaning against the trees. Soon most of the militiamen were in the high branches and, like ripe fruit, ready for the picking.

Yip, Yip, Yip, Yip, Yip! The Cherokees' war whoop stunned the white men. The howling braves sprang from the woods, shooting arrows at the men in the trees. A dozen soldiers fell on the first volley, hitting the ground with heavy thuds. The Indians picked up the rifles and bludgeoned the soldiers with tomahawks as they tried to escape.

Sequoyah saw one militiaman reach his horse and ride for the stream. Sequoyah jumped into the stream after the soldier. He could swim swiftly, so his lame leg didn't hold him back. On the other side of the water, another brave caught the man, leaping on his horse from behind. The Indian pulled his knife. The soldier grabbed the brave's arm, and the two struggled fiercely. The militiaman got the better of the brave, hurling him to the ground and grabbing his knife. The soldier leaped from his horse and took the brave by the neck. As he was about to cut the Indian's throat, Sequoyah reached them, pulled out his knife, and pushed the long blade into the soldier's side. The man fell backward, moaning in agony. Sequoyah kneeled over him and plunged his knife into the man's chest, killing him.

Sequoyah started back across the stream to rejoin the fight. But the grateful brave, whose life Sequoyah had saved, called him back. He began sawing the dead man's scalp away with his knife, showing the young Sequoyah how it was done.

All around the site of the battle, the braves were scalping their victims. There was great glory in showing off scalps after a battle, but the time it took to collect them was costly. It required at least two minutes to take a scalp, and by the time they were through, at least half of the soldiers had escaped.

When the brave handed Sequoyah the hank of hair from the man he had killed, Sequoyah felt proud. Then he looked up and saw that the rest of the white men had gotten away. The rest of the braves were jubilant. They clapped Sequoyah on the shoulders. He was now *outacite*, which means "man killer." His lameness had not stopped him from becoming a warrior.

That evening the braves mounted the scalps on poles of new pine and placed them around the fire. Whooping and screaming, they danced the scalp dance. But Sequoyah felt uneasy. He figured the white men who had escaped would surely alert the rest of the militia. Then the soldiers would storm through the Cherokee villages again, burning and killing, to repay the Indians for these injuries.

The next day a Cherokee messenger came to the village. He had some bad news. Among the soldiers who had escaped the night before was none other than the man who had shot Old Tassel. Sequoyah looked down at the scalp hanging on his belt. He felt foolish wearing it now. If he had not paused to take it, perhaps he could have found that man and avenged his uncle's death.

Sure enough, the white militiamen did come to take their own revenge. They rode into the overhill towns by the hundreds, looting and burning everything in their path. Sequoyah had moved Wu Teh to a town in the southern part of the nation to keep her safe. Many other braves had moved their families as well. But the houses and the fields could not be moved to escape the soldiers' torches.

The new fighting raged on for years. Dragging Canoe convinced 1,000 Creeks to fight alongside the Cherokees, bringing the size of his army to nearly 3,000 braves. This many Indians were a constant threat to the white settlers. Young Tassel and Doublehead still ached for revenge of Old Tassel's murder. They were Dragging Canoe's batallion chiefs, leading the deadly raids into the settlements.

In 1792, four years after Old Tassel's death, Dragging Canoe was killed by a soldier's bullet as he led a charge. After his death, the solidarity of the Cherokees began to fall apart. Young Tassel was next in command. Dragging Canoe had long recognized that Young Tassel was a more intelligent leader than the unpredictable Doublehead. But Doublehead would not submit so easily to his nephew's authority. The two argued constantly about strategy and tactics, and the army lost its unity.

Finally, Young Tassel planned an attack on the militia's stronghold in what is now Knoxville, Tennessee. On the morning of the attack, the Cherokees passed a small militia outpost at Cavett's Station, just outside Knoxville. Young Tassel wanted to ignore it. He knew that gunfire from the station would alert the men at the fort in Knoxville and ruin the Cherokees' surprise attack. But Doublehead insisted on attacking the outpost. He ignored Young Tassel and led his own raiders on the small station. Young Tassel had no choice but to follow.

The Cherokees met tough resistance from the small station. Five braves were killed immediately, and the volleys of musket fire kept coming. But the Cherokees outnumbered the small outpost, and soon its leader waved the white flag and a truce was made. Young Tassel and Doublehead both agreed that the lives of the people would be spared. They would be taken prisoner and traded for Cherokees who were being held in Knoxville.

When the station house door opened, out walked three men, three women, and seven children. Young Tassel ordered the people taken prisoner, according to the agreement. But Doublehead changed his mind. He had always been unpredictable, but lately he was almost crazed. He leaped at the first man and buried his tomahawk in his face. His raiders did likewise to the other two men. Then Doublehead and his men began killing the women and the children, even as they screamed and pleaded. By the time Young Tassel realized what was being done, only one child remained standing, a little boy. Young Tassel rushed to Doublehead's side and grabbed his hand, which was poised above the boy, gripping a dagger. Young Tassel held the older man off long enough for other warriors to carry the boy to safety. Doublehead was furious.

Sequoyah could not believe what he had seen. His eyes welled up with tears. First his "revenge" on the white men had allowed Old Tassel's killer to escape. Now revenge had brought his other uncle to madness and senseless slaughter of innocent people. Sequoyah began to doubt the wisdom of this war. Just because Old

Tassel was dead, he thought, didn't mean his dream of peace should die also. Sequoyah began to feel that the need for revenge was making the Cherokees men who no longer kept their word. He had thought only white men were like that.

Things went poorly for the Cherokees after that. John Sevier, the militia captain, led a force of 600 men across the Tennessee River after the Cherokees, seeking revenge for the killings at Cavett's Station. Young Tassel dug in with his braves at the town of Etowah. When Sevier's forces arrived, they tricked the Cherokees out of their hiding places with scouts. When the Cherokees appeared, the militiamen shot the Indians. Even though the Cherokees greatly outnumbered their enemy, they were soundly defeated by the well-armed soldiers. It was the bloodiest battle ever seen in those hills.

Word came from Philadelphia. The new "White Father," George Washington, wished to talk peace. The Cherokees were ready to listen.

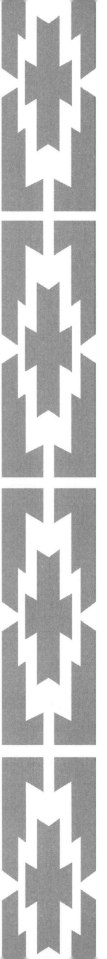

12

The Silver Peace Pipe

G eorge Washington greeted the two Cherokee chiefs warmly when they arrived at his office in Philadelphia, which was the capital of the United States at that time. The chiefs wore new, tailored suits, bought by President Washington's aides. It was the custom to provide Indians with formal clothes before admitting them to an audience with a high official.

The chiefs felt imprisoned in the stiff white collars and itchy wool trousers. But at least they didn't have to bow and kiss Washington's hand, as their fathers had done with the king of England. This new United States government had different ideas. For instance, this "Great Father" was addressed by the title "Mr. President" rather than "Your Highness."

Washington spread out a map on a polished walnut table. He pointed out the boundary line that had been drawn years ago for the Treaty of Hopewell. The boundary had been ignored by white settlers so many times before and the United States government had not been able to stop them. But now, Washington said, things would be different. In 1789 the United States had adopted a new constitution and set up a more powerful national government. Washington had been president of this new government for five years. The United States now had the power to protect the Cherokees' lands.

Washington looked up from the map. His powdered wig was pulled back and braided, exposing his strong, honest face. "Your land will be safe now forever," he said sincerely. Washington handed the chiefs a peace pipe made of pure silver, symbolizing their new understanding.

The chiefs returned to the Cherokee nation and reported Washington's promises to the council. In return for protection against the settlers taking their territory, the Cherokees were asked to learn to farm instead of hunt. The white government wanted them to eventually adopt the ways of the white people. The Cherokees agreed to this. It seemed that, short of dying, they could not avoid the New Way. At least this way they would be able to keep their land. In 1794 a new treaty was signed at Holston, Tennessee.

Sequoyah was pleased by the new treaty. He had shown himself to be a brave warrior in the recent war and his lame leg had not hampered him as he feared it would. But the revenge he sought was bitter when he tasted it. He understood now why Old Tassel had wanted peace with the white people. There was no other way.

After 1794 things began to change more quickly than ever before among the Cherokees. They gave the Americans permission to build a road through Cherokee territory, so that settlers heading for the western lands could pass through. Now there were always white people in the nation.

There were many other changes, as well, especially in the overhill towns to the north. The white people who came to teach farming encouraged Cherokees to farm a different way. The Indians were asked to abandon their communal vegetable fields in town. They went into the forest, cut down trees, and cleared out large fields. They built large farmhouses, like those of the white people, with two stories and board roofs and even brick chimneys. They also grew large orchards of apples and peaches, and kept cattle in fenced-in fields.

Soon each family had a farm that was larger than the whole town's communal field had been. The women had previously taken care of the crops when there was just one crop that everyone shared. Now the men found that they had to stay home and help their wives farm. They no longer had time to hunt.

As the men turned to farming, the women took up other skills from the white people. They learned how to use the spinning wheel, to spin cotton thread from fresh-grown cotton, and to weave the thread into clothing.

All in all, the Cherokees found this new way of life more profitable than the old. One man, returning home from a long hunt, saw that the cloth his wife had made while he was gone was worth more than the skins he had been able to gather in six months. The new abundance of corn, tobacco, and other crops brought even more money.

Many Indians also began to send their children to the white schools. Missionaries came into the Cherokee nation and taught youngsters to read and write in English. Some of the children went on to white high schools and colleges outside of Cherokee country.

While many Indians took easily to the white people's ways, there were others who felt out of place. These Cherokees refused to clear the forests and build farms. They clustered in the villages and stubbornly hung on to their old communal lives. This was especially true in the southern towns of the Chickamaugans, who were always the most resistant to change. In those towns, it was as if history was marching through and passing the Cherokees by. The people became frustrated. Some could not accept the New Way of the white people. But there were no longer enough animals for them to live as hunters had in the past. In their frustration, many of these Indians turned to drink. The white men's whiskey was readily available in Cherokee country, even though it was illegal to sell it to the Indians. Some chose to drink as a way to escape a changing world they could not understand.

In 1803 the new president, Thomas Jefferson, thought he had a solution to the problems of the dissatisfied Cherokees. He had just bought the Louisiana Territory, which doubled the size of the young United States. This territory added millions of acres of land west of the Mississippi River all the way to the Rocky Mountains. Jefferson offered the unhappy Chickamaugans land in the Western territories to settle on. Here they could continue their old hunting lifestyle. More than 1,000 accepted. They moved to the Arkansas Territory and became known as the Western Cherokees.

Around the same time, Jefferson made a deal with the young state of Georgia. He said he would eventually pursuade the rest of the Cherokees to leave their land in the east, land which Georgia claimed for itself. In return, Georgia would give its western holdings to the federal government. Jefferson saw these and other new western territories as the solution to the "Indian problem." There were many Indians, like the Cherokees, living in the east. The government was trying to "civilize" them. Jefferson was sure most of these Indians would eventually wish to move west, where the game for hunting was plentiful. Now that the United States owned land for them to move to, Jefferson was sure they would one day accept it. The western territories soon became known as "Indian Territory," as more and more tribes relocated there, by choice or by force.

But most of the Cherokees were changing quicker than anyone expected. Not only did they become farmers and send their children to school, but they also began to organize their government like the white people's. They stopped the old system of *lex talionis*, or "an eye for an eye" justice. Instead they chose sheriffs in every district who were responsible for enforcing laws.

When it began to look as if the Cherokees might not move west quite so willingly, Jefferson took precautions. He told the government trading agents to give the Cherokees credit for any goods they wished to buy. When it came time to pay up and the Cherokees had no money, the government would be justified in asking for payment in land. This happened time and again, and the Cherokees' land holdings continued to shrink.

Several years after the Treaty of Holston was signed, Wu Teh passed away, leaving Sequoyah alone in the world. Wu Teh hadn't been happy since Old Tassel's murder. Both of her brothers, Doublehead and Pumpkin Boy, were killed by men from their own tribe, and she grew more and more withdrawn. Many thought Doublehead deserved what he got. He had been irresponsible during the war, and he had tried to rob the Cherokees after the war. Wu Teh spent her last years mourning her dead brothers. Her only happiness was Sequoyah, for he seemed to prosper no matter what happened to the Cherokees.

Taskigi began to look more and more like a white settlement with the farms outside of town and Indians dressed in white people's clothes. In fact it was hard to tell who was an Indian and who was a white settler. More than ever before, Sequoyah guarded his Indian ways. He dressed as an Indian, in a homespun shirt with a scarf tied at the neck, a flowing robe, turban, buckskin vest, and leggings. And though his business often brought him in contact with white men, he stubbornly refused to learn English.

But Sequoyah prospered right along with the other Cherokees. He had always worked well with his hands and with tools, and he learned to be a blacksmith easily. He made his own bellows and forge, and earned a good living patching copper pots, balancing wagon wheels, and repairing muskets. He also began to melt down silver coins and hammer them into bracelets and earrings. On some of the flattened silver he drew pictures and designs. Sequoyah soon became known as a fine silversmith too.

Sequoyah's silver jewelry was so much in demand that traders encouraged him to stamp his wares with a trademark. Sequoyah persuaded an English-speaking friend, George Hicks, to write out his name in English. Hicks mistakenly wrote out "George Guess" instead of "George Gist," Sequoyah's white name. But Sequoyah couldn't tell the difference. He cast his name as his friend had written it into his trademark stamp. Silver jewelry and other wares made by Sequoyah can still be found with the trademark "George Guess" stamped into them.

When Sequoyah looked at his new trademark, the letters stirred his memory. He thought of his old project, to write down the talk of the Cherokees. Now, more than ever, he wanted to find a way to write down the speech of his people. It needed to be done before the white teachers taught all the Cherokee children to speak and read English. But when Sequoyah looked at the town and the farmhouses with their smoking chimneys, and the children going off to school, he felt that perhaps it was already too late.

* * *

Sequoyah began to feel confined in Taskigi. He packed his things in a wagon and moved south, to a town called Willstown, in what is now Alabama. The white men's changes hadn't come to Willstown yet. People still lived in a village there, as they once had in Taskigi. And there was still game to be found in the forests.

In Willstown, Sequoyah settled down. He married a woman named Sally and built a large cabin there. They were happy. His wife worked in the communal fields, raising the "three sisters" of the Cherokees—corn, beans, and squash—and Sequoyah did his blacksmithing work. Over the years, their family tree blossomed. First they had a baby boy, then a girl, then another boy, and another.

But the changes in the Cherokee nation reached Willstown too. Soon a mission school was built nearby, and the children of the town were learning English.

One night, in 1809, Sequoyah sat down to dinner in the home of his wife's sister. Sequoyah was thirty-nine now. There were creases in his forehead and around his eyes. He was an established man now, with a large family of his own. He puffed almost continuously on a long-stemmed pipe.

Sequoyah's children were seated around the fire along with their cousins. The venison stew had been eaten and the men were lighting their pipes. Sequoyah's six-year-old nephew sat down at his elbow and showed him a book. It was a slim "speller," a book containing all the letters of the English alphabet. Sequoyah's nephew was using the book in his class at the mission school. The child smiled as Sequoyah scanned page after page, absorbed in the curious markings.

Sally stood nearby. Sequoyah's wife was a dark-skinned woman with long, black, braided hair. She was a full-blood Cherokee, but she had more patience than her husband for accepting the white people's ways.

"It is good," Sally said. "The child will learn to put down the talk."

Sequoyah stared quietly at the pages. Suddenly, he clapped the book closed and looked into the fire. His mind raced. He remembered white men trailing through his country, and he thought of Old Tassel, lying dead with a white flag in his hand. Sequoyah looked down at his nephew and thought of the words of Dragging Canoe, long, long ago. "Do we need the white man to chew our food for us and stuff it in our beaks, like we are helpless baby sparrows?"

Sequoyah stood, his eyes aglow with firelight. "They will never be satisfied," he cried. "They will feed the worm to us." Sequoyah grabbed the speller and hurled it into the fire. His nephew started to cry. Sally, her eyes wide, snatched the book from the fire and put out the small flame that had burned the corner. "A witch has entered you," she shouted.

Sequoyah ignored her. "We can put down *our* talk," he stormed. "We do not need the white man to force his talk into our mouths."

Sally laughed. "Who will put down our talk then?" she asked. "It is only for the white men to make talking leaves. Even a child knows that."

The rest of the evening, Sequoyah stared into the fire, puffing his pipe without saying a word. The little children circled around him. They weren't sure whether they should talk to him or not. Sequoyah didn't notice them. He watched the leaping flames, which seemed to mirror his thoughts. He knew what he must do.

13
A Thing to Be Built

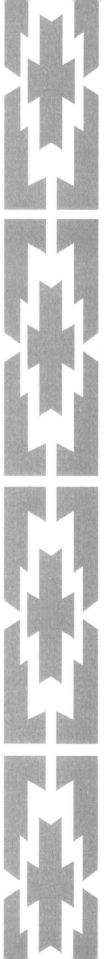

Later that night, Sequoyah dug through a basket in a forgotten corner of his cabin. He pulled out the book that had been wrapped in cloth for more than twenty years, since the day Old Tassel was murdered. He unwrapped the cloth. The chips of bark he had worked on back then fell to the dirt floor.

Sequoyah picked up the bark and looked at the scratchings on them. He felt the same excitement he did as a teenager, when he had first thought of drawing the Cherokee talk. Even then Sequoyah had such confidence in himself that he had decided to try it. He thought he could build anything! Now Sequoyah was even more accomplished and his confidence was stronger than ever.

Sequoyah looked at his hands. He had used those talented hands to put images from his mind onto silver.

He could bend and reshape iron wheels on his anvil. He was a master craftsman. Surely, if anyone could draw the talk of the Cherokees, it would be he.

Sequoyah knew it would not be easy, but he would treat it as any other job. He built a small cabin in the woods near his home. Every night after his blacksmithing work was done, he went to the small cabin, lit a lamp, and sat down to work on drawing the Cherokee talk. He did not know the word "writing," since the Cherokees did not have a written language. He also had no idea of the challenge he faced as he sat puffing his long-stemmed pipe and musing over the pieces of bark that would be his notepaper.

Sequoyah began as he had many years before. He tried to draw a picture, or symbol, to represent each word in the Cherokee language. He soon saw that this would be too difficult. It wasn't a matter of merely drawing a picture of every person, place, or thing—in other words, every noun. For one thing, there were also verbs, words that represent actions. How could he draw pictures of verbs or actions? And how was it possible to draw adjectives, the words that describe things? How would he show something was "perfect" or "ugly" or "silly" with a picture. Then there was the problem of abstract nouns, things that are not visible, such as "courage" or "power."

Sequoyah's task grew larger and larger the longer he sat and puffed his pipe and thought about it. He must have felt as if he had agreed to count every single grain of sand on a beach. But when he actually carved out his symbols, he felt better. He had always liked the feel of his knife and a piece of wood in his hands. Soon he had piled up a number of symbols.

The symbols that Sequoyah made are called "ideograms." *Ideo* means "idea." Ideograms are pictures of ideas, as well as things. Many languages of the world have used ideograms. The characters in the Chinese language, for example, were originally ideograms.

Some ideograms are easy to recognize. For example, the Chinese character that looks like a simply drawn tree means "tree."

The character that looks like a sun means "sun." Combinations of symbols are used to represent ideas. The Chinese express "east" by combining the symbols for sun and tree into a picture of the sun rising behind a tree. If one remembers that the sun rises from the east, the symbol works.

Sequoyah made many such ideograms for Cherokee words. As he worked, it became obvious that it would require a great many symbols to represent all of the words in Cherokee. In Sequoyah's day white people thought that Indian languages had only two or three hundred words. In fact, the Cherokee language had more than twenty thousand words, as did most Indian languages.

Sometimes Sequoyah would stop carving and reflect on his enormous task. He thought he could make anything. But to draw the Cherokee talk was something different. Usually when he carved, he held one image in his mind and put it in the silver or wood. But there were hundreds and thousands of images contained in the Cherokee language! He had to find a way to represent them all. It made him stretch his mind in ways he had never done before. Sequoyah worked on, night after night in his candle-lit cabin. Symbol after symbol piled up on the packed dirt floor.

From time to time Sally walked outside in the moonlight and saw the light burning in Sequoyah's cabin. He seldom sat by their fire after dinner anymore, telling stories and smoking his pipe. He seemed possessed. "Well," she thought, "it *is* crazy, but at least he is not out drinking whiskey like so many of the other men these days. At least he does his work when the sun is up, and keeps this foolishness to himself at night. Soon he will grow tired of it."

Sally turned out to be right, at least for a while. Sequoyah began to grow frustrated with his huge project. He was accustomed to finishing the tasks he started, but he had never done anything like this before. It was impossible to say when he would be finished. He didn't even know what to call what he was doing, besides "drawing talk."

Often Sequoyah felt he was nearing completion, then some chance idea reminded him of a word he had forgotten, then another. Then he'd remember whole sets of ideas he had left out. It was maddening. All the while the pieces of bark with symbols written on them piled higher and higher. It was frustrating to work night after night, with no end in sight, and no encouragement from anyone.

After a while Sequoyah spent fewer and fewer nights working in his cabin. He still went there, on odd nights, to carve out some symbol or set of words he realized he had left out. But other interests also became important during the next few years. Eventually, the stack of symbols carved in bark lay untouched on the cabin floor, gathering dust under tents of cobwebs.

𝕽𝕽𝕽𝕽𝕽 **14** 𝕽𝕽𝕽𝕽𝕽

A Voice From Long Ago

S equoyah sat among the noisy crowd gathered outside the council house in Tuckabatchee, in the country of the Creeks. Indians from many different tribes had come that evening to hear a speech by the great Tecumseh, the fiery leader of the Shawnees. Sequoyah was excited to be there. His life had grown humdrum. This was just the tonic he needed—excitement.

Everyone grew quiet as the dancers surrounded the fire. They were naked, except for breechcloths and deerskin moccasins. They danced a wild, circling dance, full of violent movements that suggested war. One of the dancers turned out to be none other than Tecumseh.

After the dance, Tecumseh stood in front of the crowd and opened his arms, palms out. Then he began to speak. "I have come to tell you how things were in old times," he said. Sequoyah was reminded of a similar night, many years before, when Cornstalk had spoken to the Cherokees. Tecumseh's message was very much the same.

"You must give up your mills and your houses, kill your cats, and discard all the fashions of the white men," Tecumseh said. "You must return to the Old Way."

Tecumseh called on all Indian tribes to unite against America, who would soon be at war with Britain again. The British army would come back and help the united Indians defeat the white men once and for all.

Most of the Cherokees present were angered. They remembered too well the fate of their tribe the last time this message was brought to them. Dragging Canoe had begun a war that eventually involved their entire nation, and that war was in vain. The white people were too numerous to defeat. Peace was the only way— peace and acceptance of the New Way.

Many of the Creeks there felt the same. They wished to continue on the path to peace. Sequoyah agreed, too, but he couldn't help being moved by Tecumseh's speech. The Shawnee chief's words rang true, just as the words of Cornstalk and Dragging Canoe rang true so many years before. But they were the words of an idealist and not practical. As much as the Cherokees might wish to return to the Old Way, it was impossible. Many among them had tried it once and failed.

Sequoyah was convinced that Tecumseh, noble and well spoken as he seemed, was in error. The New Way was real. The Old Way was merely a dream. The white people could not be defeated. Sequoyah thought of his project. He saw it again as a chance to give the Cherokees a New Way that was not the white man's way. If he could write down the Cherokees' talk, their children would not have to go to the white men's schools and learn English. Laws could be written in Cherokee, not English. The tales of their old medicine men, who were beginning to die off, could be captured in the marks on talking leaves and saved for the children of the nation, and their children.

Sequoyah's mind was ablaze as he listened to Tecumseh. He, Sequoyah, had the real answer for his people, not this young prophet. Sequoyah thought of telling the people gathered there about his project, to make them see that his was a better plan. Then he thought of his little cabin, where the pieces of bark were strewn on the floor, covered in cobwebs. Sequoyah felt ashamed. He had left his most important job unfinished.

Many of the Indians present that night thought Tecumseh's plan was a good one. A group of young Creeks, too young to remember Dragging Canoe and Cornstalk, were carried away by Tecumseh's emotional speech. This group was called the Red Sticks. They wanted to defeat the white men and any Indians who followed the New Way. So they sided with the British against the United States in what was called the War of 1812.

The Cherokees responded to the challenge of the Red Sticks. They took sides with the United States, along with many of the older Creek warriors. These Indians felt that if they fought the United States again, like the foolish Red Sticks, they would end up with no land at all. But if they helped the United States defeat the Red Sticks and the British, their chances of keeping their remaining land would be good.

Sequoyah was more than forty years old when the War of 1812 started, but he was not about to let his age keep him from fighting alongside his people.

When Sequoyah showed up to enlist in the Cherokee regiment, the young officer saw his limp and laughed. "This ain't a hospital, it's an army. We got no use for cripples," he sneered. But an older officer recognized Sequoyah and remembered his valiant service in the last war. "That man is the nephew of Old Tassel and Doublehead, and he can fight as well as any man here, on one leg," the old officer said. The young officer blushed, and Sequoyah was allowed to enlist.

The Cherokees fought bravely in the war, especially at the battle of Horseshoe Bend. General Andrew Jackson was in command of the United States troops during that battle. Jackson was called "Ol' Hickory" by his troops because of his tough nature. His batallion at Horseshoe Bend was trapped in the forest by Creek warriors. Meanwhile, the Cherokees moved up the Tallapoosa River behind the Creeks, and silently stole the canoes the Creeks planned to use in their escape. The Cherokees paddled downriver in those same canoes and came up on the Creeks from the other side. The Creeks were surprised and defeated easily.

The Cherokees had saved the lives of many of their United States allies, but neither the soldiers nor Jackson were grateful. Many of the soldiers were from Tennessee, Kentucky, and North Carolina, and still remembered the settlers' wars against the Cherokees. Now, riding through Cherokee territory on their way home, they looted and burned the towns in their path.

What's more, General Jackson asked permission from the Secretary of War to lead his regiment in an all-out war against the Cherokees and take their remaining lands from them once and for all. Fortunately, the secretary was not as ungrateful as Jackson. He angrily denied the request. But it was not the last the Indians would hear from Ol' Hickory.

* * *

When Sequoyah returned home after being away for more than a year, he found his house and grounds in bad need of repair. The roof on his cabin leaked, the fields were overgrown with weeds, and the fences in the hog yard and the chicken coop needed mending. Sequoyah had already decided to get down to work as soon as he got home, but not mending fences and fixing roofs. That could wait. He had important work to do.

Sequoyah had been thinking night and day of Tecumseh's speech, how it lit a fire in the hearts of the Red Sticks. Tecumseh had been wrong about going to war. But he had been right about

98

one thing. The Indians must not give up everything for the white men. Sequoyah saw that his project was important, not just for the Cherokees, but for all Indians. Tecumseh had shown him that his concerns about the Cherokee way of life and language were shared by Indians everywhere. Sequoyah only hoped that he was equal to the great task that lay before him.

Before he went to war, Sequoyah worked only at night on his symbols. Now he worked night and day in the little cabin. He even slept there, curled up in a blanket on the floor. Sequoyah was determined. He decided that the time had come to complete his work, before he grew too old. He was already almost forty-five. Who knew how long he would be given.

But Sally grew more and more impatient with her husband. For more than a year she had taken care of the children and run the household by herself, while Sequoyah was off fighting—and at his age! Now that he was back he spent all his time in his cabin, scraping foolish pictures on pieces of bark. Sally was tired of going to the doorway of the little cabin and shouting at her husband, "Fix the fence, patch the roof, you lazy bear." Sequoyah was too good at ignoring pleas like this. He would simply turn away from her, relight his pipe, and calmly blow a few blasts of smoke. Sally was furious and wouldn't take this silent treatment for long. She was determined to end Sequoyah's foolishness. And she thought she knew just how to do it.

One evening while Sequoyah was away getting water from the stream, Sally put her plan into effect. She lit a pine notch and threw it on the roof of Sequoyah's little cabin. The fire quickly ate through the dried bark of the roof, and soon the walls came crashing down in flames. When Sequoyah returned, the blaze was burning fiercely, out of control.

Sequoyah took the buckets of water he was carrying and heaved them on the fire, but it did no good. The cabin burned quickly and soon it was a mere pile of smoking ruins. Sequoyah grabbed a stick and stirred through the ashes, looking for his

priceless pieces of bark; but they were burnt to cinders, each and every one.

Sally found Sequoyah sitting in front of the smouldering rubble with his head in his hands. She lashed out at him. This was the end of his foolish dreaming. He must now wake up and see the sunlight. There was work to be done.

Sequoyah didn't even seem angry with his wife. He simply sat and listened to her voice. It was as if he was hearing the Cherokee language spoken for the first time.

Sequoyah suddenly felt a queer sense of freedom. He was almost happy that his symbols had gone up in smoke. Sally's harsh words seemed like a melody to him. He wasn't paying attention to what she was saying but to what the words sounded like. There was something curious about the sounds of words, he thought. The same ones seem to show up, again and again. He looked up at Sally, and through the tears in his eyes, he smiled.

Talk Is Made of Sounds

After Sequoyah returned from the war, he and Sally had another child, a baby girl they named Ayokeh. When her daughter was born, Sally hugged her close and whispered to her, "Baby, I am sorry you were not born before your father became possessed by witches. He was a good man in the old days."

Sally had almost given up all hope for Sequoyah. He hadn't reacted at all when she burned down his cabin. She had expected to light a fire under Sequoyah as well. She had hoped to get him thinking more about work and less about his silly dreams. Instead, Sequoyah was dreamier than ever.

One day Sequoyah went to the home of his wife's sister. He asked his nephew if he could borrow his spelling book, the one with the English alphabet in it. By this time, the boy had forgotten that his uncle once threw the speller into the fire. The boy was even happy to read a few of the characters to him. The boy opened the book and pointed to the first letter. "A," the boy said. "That sounds like this, 'Ah.' "

"Ah," said Sequoyah.

Then Sequoyah wanted to know how many words this sound could be used in. The boy brightened, proud to show off his knowledge. "Well, there's star and jar and far and . . ." The boy paused for a minute, then his eyes grew wide. He smiled and said, ". . . and tar."

Sequoyah had heard all he wanted to hear for now. He patted his nephew on the head, tucked the speller under his arm, and was off.

Sequoyah's nephew didn't have a chance to tell his uncle that the "A" had more than one sound. But Sequoyah had heard enough. His suspicions about the letters in the white people's alphabet were correct. They were "cages" that held *sounds*, not ideas.

Sequoyah began work on a new cabin. This time it was deep in the woods, a long walk from his home. When it was finished, he took no chances. He kept a big dog there, to protect the place.

One day Sally made her way through the woods to peek at the new cabin, and what she saw made her sad. She found Sequoyah sitting in front of the cabin under the tall trees with a vacant look on his face. He seemed to be listening. "What is he trying to hear?" Sally wondered. "The birds chirping in the trees? Maybe they talk to him," she thought sarcastically. Then she saw him say something softly to himself and repeat it over and over again. "So," she thought, "if the birds don't talk to him, he talks to himself. Some husband I've got!"

From time to time, Sequoyah's face brightened. Then he began scratching and carving on a piece of bark. "The poor fool," thought Sally. "A witch has got hold of him, that is sure."

Sequoyah was also acting peculiarly at home. He began entertaining guests, usually hopeless ne'er do wells who'd become common in the town. They'd drain Sequoyah's whiskey barrels and talk and talk and talk. Sequoyah seldom drank anything. He merely sat and listened to his tipsy, talkative friends with a faint glow of approval in his smiling eyes. Sometimes he repeated what someone had just said. But he would say each word in pieces, dividing it into separate sounds. After doing this, he would sometimes scratch out a mark on a piece of bark.

He did the same thing everywhere he went. When Sequoyah passed through town, he would stop and chat with everyone. But he always had a faraway look in his eyes, as if he were listening to something besides what was being said.

After a while, some of the people in the town got worried and went to Sally. "Your husband is surely possessed by a demon witch," they said. Sally agreed, but she didn't know what should be done.

Finally, one day while Sequoyah sat in front of his cabin, listening and making strange noises to himself and drawing on his barks, Sally brought the medicine man. The medicine man, wearing a frightful mask, began chanting a strange, moody hymn. He circled the cabin, kicking out his right leg, then his left, and shaking his gourd rattle.

While the medicine man circled the cabin, Sequoyah went on scratching. Suddenly, Sequoyah looked up from his barks and listened intently. He seemed to hear something in the medicine man's song. After a moment, he went back to scratching at the bark, even more furiously than before. Then he stood up, lit his pipe, calmly blew out some smoke, and went into the cabin. The medicine man threw up his hands and went home.

Inside the cabin, Sequoyah added the pieces of bark to the growing pile of new symbols. When Sally burned down his first cabin, destroying all of his old work, he had actually been relieved. He had suspected for some time that the method he was using wouldn't work. There were too many Cherokee words to make pictures of all of them. He had needed a new plan.

Although Sequoyah had been angry with Sally, he reasoned, "You can destroy bark, but you can't destroy talk. Talk travels on the wind and cannot be burned. Talk is not made of wood. Talk is made of sound."

Sound! Of course.

Sequoyah had been shocked by this new insight. He scolded himself. It was so obvious, a child could have seen it. Talk is made of sound!

Sequoyah had been trying to make symbols for all of the words and ideas of his language. Then he realized that he only had to write down the *sounds* that words are made of. For no matter how many words and ideas a language has, there are only a limited number of sounds and each sound is repeated in many, many different words.

Others who had created writing systems had come to the same conclusion Sequoyah did. The Phoenicians used an ideographic writing system for hundreds of years. Then, around 1,000 B.C., they decided to use their symbols to represent sounds rather than ideas. The new system worked so well that in the following century, the Greeks adopted many of the Phoenician symbols for their own alphabet. Eventually, many of these characters became part of the alphabet of the English language.

The Chinese, too, eventually decided to use their symbols to represent sounds instead of whole words. But it also took them a long time to come to this conclusion. Sequoyah, working with his knife and his barks, made the same discovery in a tiny fraction of the time. And he did it all alone, with only a hint from his nephew's spelling book.

By listening carefully to his fellow Cherokees when they talked and by repeating the words, Sequoyah gradually developed an ear for the different sounds in his language. He noticed that each word seemed to break down into separate units of sound, or *syllables*. Each syllable can be broken down further into letters, or an *alphabet*, but Sequoyah stopped at the syllable. He made a symbol for each sound, or syllable. Sequoyah created a *syllabary*.

Sequoyah began to think of the sounds of the Cherokee language as wild things, to be hunted and captured in the symbols he created. Then they could be made to work for the Cherokees, just like a tamed animal.

As Sequoyah worked, month after month, alone in his cabin in the woods, the people in town grew increasingly wary of him. There was a queer look in his eyes whenever he spoke with them. He hid in his cabin, day after day, seeing no one. He scratched strange pictures on pieces of bark. It was witchcraft, many said. The man was possessed by a demon witch.

But Sequoyah paid no attention to the superstitious townspeople. One day they would understand. When he had written down the Cherokee talk, he'd show his people how to make Cherokee medicine as powerful as the white people's.

Early in 1817, Sequoyah looked up from his labors and decided he had finished. He felt he had captured all the sounds in his language. He bought some parchment paper and a good quill pen at the trading post and made some ink by boiling oak leaf galls and iron filings in water. Then he copied the symbols from the chips of bark onto the paper. Sequoyah had borrowed some of these symbols from his nephew's speller. But he didn't use them for their English sounds, for he didn't know what their sounds were in English. He didn't write them in the same way the speller did. Sequoyah used these English letters to represent Cherokee sounds and made up other characters himself. In all, there were a little more than 100 characters. After Sequoyah copied them, he held up the stiff page and blew on the ink until it dried. Then he rolled the parchment into a tube and carried it home under his arm.

Sequoyah put on his best shirt and cloak, wound a fresh clean turban around his head, and went off to see John Ross, a high official in the Cherokee National Council. The Indian government was located in New Echota, the current capital of the Cherokee nation. Ross was only one-eighth Cherokee and was educated in the white people's schools. But the Indians said that in his soul he was a full-blood. He was a young man of twenty-six, with a great deal of promise. He had a college degree and could read and write English as well as many other languages. He was well respected in the nation. Sequoyah felt Ross would be the man to understand the great thing he had made. In addition, the two were old army pals. They had fought side by side in the battle of Horseshoe Bend just a few years earlier.

But Ross had heard the stories of Sequoyah's peculiar habit of sitting in the woods for days on end, talking to himself. Besides, Ross was a busy man. The neighboring state of Georgia was making things very difficult for the Cherokees these days. It was demanding that the United States government honor an old agreement to remove all the Indians from lands that Georgia claimed and send them to the Western territory. Ross had done all he could do to stop this horrible fate. He was working against some very powerful and greedy men. He had no time for the "games" of old Sequoyah.

Sequoyah patiently tried to explain the principles of his syllabary, but Ross saw no use for it. "Ridiculous. Our children will learn English when they want to write," he said. "This is too long; it would be impossible to learn." Ross thought that the Cherokee children were having a tough enough time learning the twenty-six characters in the English alphabet.

Ross politely excused himself. He had work to do. He thanked Sequoyah for taking the time to show him his "hobby," but he really didn't think it was practical.

Sequoyah walked away angry. He thought of Ross in his starched white collar and tie, his white man's trousers, and leather shoes. "This college boy," thought Sequoyah, "won't even try to understand my work because he thinks it's too hard to learn." Sequoyah was determined to show Ross how wrong he was.

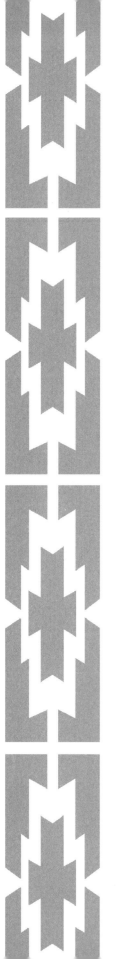

🜪🜪🜪🜪🜪 **16** 🜪🜪🜪🜪🜪

A Trip to the West

In 1817 Sequoyah traveled by flatboat along the Tennessee, Ohio, Mississippi, and Arkansas rivers to the home of the Cherokee Nation West. He was sick of the constant conflict in the eastern settlements. The white missionaries tried to "civilize" the Cherokees while the white lawmakers of Georgia tried to take their land from them. To make matters worse, he and Sally were always bickering. When he suggested they take a vacation to the western part of the Cherokee nation, she replied, "Why don't you vacate yourself." And so he left.

Sequoyah stepped off the boat and looked out at his new home. Before him was a vast, flat plain of shaggy marsh grass, with an occasional tree here and there. The land was not as pretty as his country back East. But at least the whites weren't always badgering the Indian people here to leave.

Sequoyah set up in a little cabin near a salt flat and got right back to work on his syllabary. He felt like a fool for having gone to Ross with only a sheet of squiggly lines. Of course the man thought he was a fool! Who wouldn't? Sequoyah realized that before anyone could recognize the worth of his syllabary, he would have to show them that it *worked*.

Sequoyah was also angry with himself for rushing to show Ross his work before it was perfected. As soon as he left Ross, he saw that some of his symbols were repetitive. In many cases, he had made two symbols where only one would do.

Sequoyah worked every evening in his cabin, saying the sounds aloud again and again, and removing unnecessary symbols. Soon he had cut the number down to around ninety-four symbols. Sequoyah's syllabary was still not as compact as the English alphabet, but in other ways it was far easier to learn. Each letter of the English alphabet has many sounds. In Sequoyah's syllabary each character has only one sound.

The word "expediency" contains five different syllables. In English, these syllables are made up of several letters, each of which may be pronounced in many ways. In Cherokee, the word would be written with five characters only, one for each sound. It would appear something like: X-P-D-N-C.

When Sequoyah felt that he had perfected his syllabary, he invited people over to look at it. He carefully explained how his invention worked and tried to teach it to his friends, slowly and patiently. He felt that if someone besides himself could master the syllabary, Ross and the other head men of the tribe in New Echota would see its value.

Sequoyah found only a couple of friends willing to learn the syllabary. So far no one had accused him of witchcraft, as the people in the East had done. His friends resisted his teaching at first, but soon they were glad to learn. Eventually, they took great pleasure in writing notes to each other and reading them.

Sequoyah developed a regular fan club among the Western Cherokees. A group of people saw the value of what he had done and encouraged him to travel back East and try again to convince the Cherokee National Council that his invention worked. Sequoyah decided to take their advice. But this time, he would do it differently.

No one was confident enough to return to New Echota with Sequoyah to face the examination the chiefs were sure to put them through. His pupils were still confused by some of the symbols. In fact, Sequoyah was, too, sometimes. So he had each of them dictate a letter to a friend in the Cherokee Nation East. Sequoyah wrote these letters using his syllabary and read them back to his astonished admirers. Then he rolled up the letters, slid them into his pack, and set out for the East.

When Sequoyah returned to Willstown in 1821, he had been gone for four years. Nevertheless, he was still greeted by laughter and catcalls in the street. "Ah, the witch is back," many said. "Have you cast a spell on the Cherokees in the west?" others sneered.

Sequoyah returned to his old home. Sally was still suspicious of his work. She was cold to him, treating him as if he were a fool who would never contribute to their family. The only person who was glad to see Sequoyah was his little daughter, Ayokeh. Her bright, cheerful eyes and raven hair were the same features Sequoyah had loved in her mother years ago. But Ayokeh was the only joy he had upon returning home.

At first Sequoyah was reluctant to go to the National Council in New Echota. If his own townspeople ridiculed him, the sophisticated chiefs in the capital would be even crueler. He felt he must teach his syllabary to someone else to prove to the chiefs that it worked.

Sequoyah spent day after day in his little cabin off in the woods, trying to think of someone who might consent to learn his syllabary. His daughter Ayokeh often visited him there, and she became interested in the strange marks on his sheets of parchment. Little by little, Sequoyah explained them to her. To his astonishment, she caught on quickly. Within a week, she had learned them all and was beginning to write them out. Seqouyah could not believe his luck. He needed someone to learn his syllabary, and that someone had come to him, out of nowhere. And it was his own little daughter too.

What's more, Ayokeh pointed out many duplications in the syllabary that were confusing. She showed her father where some of the characters could be combined into a single sign. Sequoyah saw the genius of her corrections right away and trimmed his syllabary down to eighty-six characters. Now he was confident of his invention. He packed his papers and left for New Echota with Ayokeh.

17

Final Exam

Sequoyah was tense as he stood in the council room before a round table where the head men of the tribe sat watching him and waiting. They were busy men. They had agreed to hear Sequoyah only after his old friend Agi Li had convinced them that "it could do no harm." Agi Li was half-white and had been educated in the white schools. His white name was George Lowery, and he was now a respected chief himself. If not for him, Sequoyah may never have gotten this chance. Sequoyah knew he must not fail now, for Agi Li's sake.

Sequoyah read the letters from the Western Cherokees, some of which were addressed to men in the room. One was to a Major Ridge and his son John Ridge, and another was to the old principal chief, Pathkiller. There was even a letter for John Ross. When he had finished, Sequoyah looked up at the stern faces of the men sitting around the table. They were not convinced.

"Those are very fine sentiments, Sequoyah," Ross said. "But, as you well know, this proves nothing. You could have made all this up yourself. Really, we have more important things . . ."

At that moment, Ayokeh stepped into the room. The men were taken off guard. Ross, however, was angry. "Really, Sequoyah," he said, "this is no place for children."

Sequoyah lifted his hand to hush Ross. "Wise chiefs, this is my daughter, who has learned the arts I speak of," he said proudly.

The men began to talk among themselves. "Well," they said, "if she can read what he writes, then it must work." A test was quickly set up.

Sequoyah sat down with a quill pen and a fresh piece of parchment, while Ross dictated a letter to him. Sequoyah wrote down everything Ross said using the syllabary. Then he handed the paper to Ayokeh. The room was hushed as Ayokeh rose to recite.

Ayokeh stood before the round table. The men were silent and scowling. The little girl looked over at Sequoyah nervously. He smiled at her in the same warm way that he always did, as if to say, "Do your best, that's all you can do."

Ayokeh cleared her throat and read the letter flawlessly, carefully pronouncing each word. The men were speechless. Then Pathkiller stood up. "This is good medicine," the old chief said, patting Ayokeh on top of her head. She blushed with pride.

But some of the men were still not convinced. "She looks at him before she reads," said Major Ridge. "Perhaps he makes some signs to her. This could be a trick."

"Well . . ." Ross said hesitantly, "perhaps one more test is in order." It was decided that Ross and Sequoyah would travel to the other side of town and prepare another letter. Ross would then bring it back to the council room, and see if Ayokeh could read that.

An hour later, Ross returned with the new letter he had dictated to Sequoyah. Ayokeh stood calmly before her judges this

time and read it in a clear, proud voice, without one single mistake.

The scowls on the men's faces turned to smiles. Ross himself stood up and lifted Ayokeh off the floor in a bear hug. The other men patted her on the head. Then Sequoyah was sent for.

As Sequoyah stood before the council in his humble, tattered robe and turban, with his feet showing through his deerskin moccasins, the men in their suits could not help but feel ashamed, especially Ross. He thought of himself as being so sophisticated, yet he had been blind to the value of Sequoyah's creation. He had almost deprived his nation of this wonderful gift.

Ross walked up to Sequoyah and took his hand. "I am very sorry to have doubted your great work," he said. "It will truly be a boon to our people, if only they will be able to learn it." The other men also apologized to Sequoyah and congratulated him. "You have made good medicine," old Pathkiller said again and again, patting Sequoyah on the back.

18

The Cherokee Way

Suddenly Sequoyah was a celebrity, and his invention was the talk of the nation. The syllabary spread like fire in dry leaves. Since the letters could be pronounced only one way, people learned them quickly. Some could read and write after only three days of study. Within a few weeks, the leaders of the tribe had learned Sequoyah's syllabary. Then they selected the brightest young Cherokees they could find, and Sequoyah taught the children his invention in a small schoolhouse in New Echota.

The children who learned the syllabary from Sequoyah taught their families at home. All around the nation, children were seen scratching Sequoyah's characters in the dirt, showing their fathers and mothers, their grandfathers and grandmothers, how to write down the language they had spoken all their lives. Then the syllabary began to spread outward from New

Echota as people took their pens and papers on visits to relatives. The characters were carved in trees by the roadside to tell the way, and drawn on the fronts of houses to announce the names of the people who lived inside.

In less than a year the syllabary had spread to all parts of the Eastern nation. People there began to write letters to one another. Sequoyah decided to go teach the syllabary to the Western Cherokees. Then letters could be exchanged between the eastern and western parts of the nation and all Cherokees would have a way to stay in touch with each other.

Sequoyah had other reasons for wanting to leave. The Eastern nation had made a great deal of progress in recent years, but for him it wasn't home anymore. The new buildings, the large farms, the way people dressed and talked—these were all ways of the white people. He knew his people had been forced to make these changes, but he still felt more comfortable in the wide open spaces.

Sequoyah left with Ayokeh in the spring of 1822. Sally decided to remain in the East with the other children. She and Sequoyah had had too many disagreements in the past to patch things up. She might have felt a little sheepish when her husband was suddenly transformed from a bum into a national hero. Perhaps she was still angry at him or too proud to ask his forgiveness. In any case, their marriage ended.

As Sequoyah began teaching the Western Cherokees to read and write, knowledge of his syllabary continued to spread in the Eastern nation. Samuel A. Worcester, a young missionary who came to the Cherokee nation in 1825, was stunned by the widespread literacy there. He asked the board of missions to make money available to the Cherokees for a printing press in Sequoyah's syllabary. The request was granted, and the presses were set up in New Echota. In 1828 the first issue appeared of the *Cherokee Phoenix*, a newspaper printed in both English and Cherokee. Elias Boudinot, a college-educated Cherokee, was the editor.

Now the Cherokees had a national newspaper that could report all the other advancements the Indians had made over the

years. In the fourth issue of the *Phoenix*, Boudinot began to print all the laws enacted by the Cherokee National Council as far back as 1808. These laws included the new Cherokee constitution, adopted in 1828, which modeled their young nation after the United States government.

Out West, Sequoyah was gratified when he got his first copy of the *Cherokee Phoenix* in the mail at a nearby army fort. His dream for the Cherokees was completely realized. They had taken the New Way, all right, but now it was, in a very real sense, the Cherokee Way as well. The Cherokees had taken the white people's way of life, but they had not let go of their own inner life and language. They would at least have that much to call their own.

Back in New Echota, John Ross had similar thoughts. He had doubted Sequoyah at first, but now he was completely won over by the success of the syllabary. Ross knew many languages besides Cherokee. He had studied Latin, Greek, French, and Spanish, as well as English. When he compared Sequoyah's syllabary of the

Cherokee language with English and the other languages he knew, he realized the extent of Sequoyah's gift to his people. Sequoyah had made it easy for the Cherokees to become readers and writers in a very short time, but he had done more. He had preserved the Cherokees' special way of thinking and expression, which might have been lost forever if Sequoyah hadn't found a way of writing it down.

The Cherokees lived very close to nature, and their language is filled with sensitive observations about the natural world. What's more, Cherokee nouns are more than just names. They are also descriptions of things. For example, the Cherokee word for

Shop sign in Cherokee Syllabary

118

"horse" translates roughly to "carrier of heavy things." "Flag" translates to "place to be taken care of," which is the kind of place where one would put a flag to begin with.

There is also humor in some Cherokee words. For example, the Cherokee word for "lawyer" translates to "one who argues repeatedly." And their word for "California" might have come from the days of the nineteenth-century gold rush. It means "where they find money."

As Ross studied Sequoyah's syllabary, he realized what its greatest benefit to the Cherokees might be. The syllabary enabled the Cherokees to show the world, in a dramatic way, that they were indeed civilized people who were part of the nineteenth century. They had already developed laws of their own and a democratic government, and now they could read and write. They even had their own newspaper, which they could use to spread the news of their accomplishments far and wide.

People the world over took notice. The *Cherokee Phoenix* reached readers in Europe as well as all across the United States. Ross felt certain that the days when people accused the Cherokees of being barbarians were over forever. Even the harsh officials of Georgia, who had tried to evict the "savage" Cherokees from their land, would surely have to accept the Indians as civilized neighbors now.

19

The Trail
of Tears

I n the chamber of the House of Representa-
tives in Washington, D.C., a congressman stood
speaking to his fellow lawmakers, who slumped
listlessly behind their polished mahogany desks.
The speaker paused to spit brown tobacco juice into
the brass spittoon at his feet. He wiped his mouth on
his handkerchief and continued, "We owe it to the Indians, who have attempted to become civilized, to allow them to remain on their lands." When the congressman sat down, the others hardly stirred. Another
good-natured gust of hot air, most of them thought.

The chairman banged his gavel. "The Chair recog-
izes the congressman from Georgia," he announced.

The congressman from Georgia stood. He was a
short, stout man with flushed red cheeks and long
white hair, combed straight back.

The Georgia congressman aimed his narrow eyes at the rest of the men and thundered, "Gentlemen, the great, sovereign state of Georgia owns the land we are talking about, and she will never yield an inch of her native soil to those . . . those savages." The other congressmen sat up, startled by the sheer bluster of the speaker.

"Furthermore," the congressman roared, "we demand their immediate removal, so they will no longer besmirch the good lives of our people. They are disgusting, wild savages, living on roots and wild herbs." The other men harumphed and clicked their tongues in dismay to hear of such degrading practices. "Gentlemen, our people demand that this government live up to its promises and remove the Cherokees, now and forever."

The Cherokees had thought their progress would impress the world and silence any further talk of removing them from their lands. But the opposite happened. The government of Georgia became alarmed at the thought of literate Indians as neighbors. They stepped up pressure to get rid of the Cherokees.

The Georgia congressman's description of the Cherokees as "savages, living on roots" was widely reported in newspapers. The Cherokees were furious. Soon a group of Cherokee officials was in Washington, D.C. They asked the president of the United States to declare Georgia's claim on the Cherokees' land to be false under the treaties of Hopewell and Holston. They also suggested that the president give Georgia the Florida Territory instead, in order to keep the government's bargain. President James Monroe refused. He said that eventually the Cherokees would probably have to leave their land in Georgia.

The Cherokees left the White House bitterly disappointed. That evening they saw a familiar face enter the large dining room of their hotel. It was the congressman from Georgia himself. The congressman sat directly across the table from the Cherokees, without appearing to notice them.

Sequoyah's friend George Lowery was one of the Cherokees in the dining room. They were all dressed in dignified suits of the most expensive cuts. When the waiter passed their table, Lowery pointed to a large platter of cooked carrots and said, "Waiter, would you be kind enough to bring us a plate of those *roots*. As you know, we Indians are very fond of *roots*."

The crowd in the dining room howled with laughter as Lowery took the platter of carrots and dished himself out a small portion. Each time he finished a few bites, he called to the waiter in a loud voice, "Waiter, please, more of those roots!" This set the crowd laughing, as the congressman from Georgia shrank in his seat. Unfortunately, this was the only victory the Cherokees would win from the state of Georgia.

Sequoyah, now living in Arkansas, heard of his friend's joke, but he knew there was nothing funny about what was happening to the Cherokees. Each copy of the *Cherokee Phoenix* brought Sequoyah more and more bad news about his eastern people.

John Ross became principal chief of the Cherokees in the year 1829. That same year, another man rose to power. It was Andrew Jackson. He had once asked permission to wipe out his Cherokee allies after the battle of Horseshoe Bend, and now he was president of the United States. The news couldn't have been worse for the Cherokees.

Jackson struck a hard blow at all Indians shortly after he took office. He announced to Congress that he intented to draft a law called the Indian Removal Bill. The bill required all the Indians of the Southeast to give up their lands almost immediately and relocate in the Western territory of the United States. Jackson's bill would still have to be debated, so the Cherokees had time to try to stop it. Then something happened in Cherokee country that seemed like good news.

"Gold," shouted the prospectors. "We've struck gold." Cherokee miners found a large deposit of gold in the southeastern part of their territory. Mining the gold could provide the Cherokees with some much-needed cash to fight their legal battles. It looked as if the nation had gotten a good break, just when it needed one.

But when Georgians found out there was gold on Cherokee land, they no longer restrained themselves. With President Jackson as an ally, Georgia lawmakers tried to push through their own Indian removal project. In 1830 they passed a series of outrageous laws. The laws called for Georgia to seize large parcels of Cherokee land—including the land where the gold mines were located. They also wanted to cancel out all Cherokee laws in those lands.

The Georgians attempted to overstep their rights in every way. They wrote laws that said the Cherokee government could no longer meet, and that Cherokees could be sent to prison for trying to convince other Cherokees not to relocate. Their laws stated that if a white man came onto a Cherokee's land and stole his horse or murdered his wife, the Cherokee couldn't testify against the white man in court. And the laws said that Cherokees could be arrested or shot if they were caught mining gold in the newly discovered mines.

Soon after these laws were passed, Georgians entered Cherokee land in the Southeast and took over the gold mines. They went to Cherokee homes, stole cattle and picked fights; and the Indians could do nothing about it. The courts in Georgia supported the Georgia laws, and the United States Supreme Court would not give the Cherokees a hearing. President Jackson just sat back and watched the Georgians mistreat the Cherokees.

As pressure mounted on the Eastern Cherokees, it was also applied to the Western nation. In 1828 the Western Cherokees were brought to Washington, D.C., and asked to give up their land in Arkansas. Some of the Indians had been living there for more than twenty-five years. Now the government wanted them to move farther west, to what is now Oklahoma.

Sequoyah, an honored chief by this time, was present at the meeting. He was interviewed by reporters about his syllabary. Charles Bird King painted a portrait of Sequoyah that is the only likeness of him known today. In fact, the Indians were given every hospitality on their trip to Washington, D.C., except one—they were forced to give up their land in Arkansas. After days of being pressured, they finally agreed to the land exchange. Sequoyah signed the treaty, along with the other chiefs.

In 1830 the Congress began debates on the Indian Removal Bill. Speaker after speaker condemned the Indians. But many also spoke in their defense. Senator Theodore Frelinghuysen of New Jersey delivered a moving plea for justice from the Senate floor.

> *"As the tide of our population has rolled on . . . the con-fiding Indian listened to our professions of friendship: we called him brother, and he believed us. Millions after millions he has yielded to our importunity, until we have acquired more than can be cultivated in centuries—and yet we crave more! We have crowded the tribes upon a few miserable acres on our southern frontier: it is all that is left to them of their once boundless forests: and still, like the horse-leech, our insatiated cupidity cries, give! give!"*

In spite of this plea and many like it, Congress passed the Indian Removal Bill. Now it was the law of the land, as well as of Georgia, that the Eastern Indians must leave. Soon other Indians in the Southeast gave in to the pressure to "remove." The Choc-taws, Creeks, Chickasaws, and Seminoles all signed "treaties" agreeing to leave their ancestral lands and move west. Only the Cherokees held out. Chief John Ross stuck to his position. "We will not cede one more inch of land," he said. He called on his people, in articles in the *Cherokee Phoenix*, to unite and refuse to move. "United we stand," became the Cherokees' cry.

When the Georgians saw how the Cherokees used their news-paper to maintain a united front, they seized the printing presses and arrested the staff. This action gave the Cherokees their last opening. They appealed the arrests to the United States Supreme Court. This time the court acted. Chief Justice John Marshall ruled that Georgia law had no authority in Cherokee territory, and that the newspaper staff must be released. Furthermore, Marshall ruled that treaties made by the United States with the Cherokees must be honored.

The Cherokees danced in the streets the night the decision was announced. At last their rights had been upheld in a court of law. But it was a hollow victory. President Jackson refused to enforce the decision of the Supreme Court. As president, he controlled the army, the muscle behind the law, and he scoffed at Marshall's verdict. "He made the decision, let him enforce it," the president reportedly said.

The Cherokees were bewildered. Their newspaper and their capital were closed. Their money was spent, their last legal recourse had failed, and their people were disheartened. In their darkest hour, the worst blow occurred. The United States threatened a group of chiefs into signing a treaty agreeing to removal. This was done behind the backs of Ross and the other leaders of the Cherokee nation. When the Cherokee people heard about the so-called "treaty," they all came to protest in the streets. Ross had requested that they do this to show they did not agree with the treaty and that the chiefs had acted alone. But the United States used this shameful treaty to push the heartless policy of removal through.

* * *

One day in the autumn of 1838, United States soldiers entered the towns and villages of the Cherokee nation. They forced the people out of their homes, poking bayonets at their backs. Even little children, the old, and the sick were herded like cattle. They were allowed to bring only those belongings they could gather together quickly and haul on their backs.

The soldiers stood by laughing while looters, mostly from Georgia, went through the homes and set fire to them. Then they tore down the fences to the stockyards and stole the cattle.

The soldiers forced the Cherokees at gunpoint to march across hundreds of miles of harsh country to their new "home."

Day after day, week after week, they marched with their heavy burdens, aching for food and sleep. The old and the sick soon began to die from the brutal journey. One by one, they collapsed by the roadside. Family members had to brave the bayonets to get out of line and bury their dead. When the weather turned bitter cold in winter, the marchers still had a long way to go. Many more died during the long, cold nights when they were forced to sleep out on the frozen ground.

By the time the Cherokees reached the Western territories in the spring of 1839, they were exhausted and beaten. Of the 17,000 who began the march, there were 13,000 alive. More than 4,000 Indians perished on that long, brutal march, which the Cherokees would always remember as "the trail where they cried," the trail of tears.

In Washington, D.C., the new president of the United States, Martin Van Buren, spoke to the Congress. His high collar was freshly starched and his gold cufflinks glistened. "Gentlemen," the president bellowed at rows of senators and congressmen, "the government's Indian policies have had the happiest effects."

* * *

Seventy-year-old Sequoyah would provide one more important service to his people. After all the Cherokees had arrived in the Western territory, miserable and confused, they faced even more problems. There were disagreements as to who would run the new, united Cherokee government. The old settlers of the West argued with factions of the newly arrived Cherokees from the East, who vastly outnumbered them. It looked as if the situation would never be resolved, until Sequoyah wrote a letter to the old settlers in his own syllabary.

> *"We . . . want you to come without delay, that we may talk matters over like friends and brothers . . . There is no drinking here to disturb the peace though there are upward of two thousand people on the ground. We send you these few lines as friends."*

Many think Sequoyah's diplomacy helped the disunited Cherokees settle their differences. The nation was united again in the Western territory, where the Cherokee people gradually prospered. They revived the newspaper, renaming it the *Cherokee Advocate*. And Sequoyah was awarded a pension of three hundred dollars a year for life for his invention of the syllabary.

But by this time, Sequoyah was nowhere to be found. His wandering spirit had taken over. He left for the Mexican wilderness just after the nation was reunited. Sequoyah had gone to search for a long lost band of Cherokees who reportedly lived there.

As Sequoyah rode across southern Texas and Mexico, he saw many wandering bands of Indians who had been pushed out of their homes to roam these parched deserts. He thought of how the white people had robbed them of their land and lives. Sequoyah

wondered if it might be possible to develop an Indian language that all Indians could read and write, not just the Cherokees. He felt that these lost souls deserved at least that—the ability to keep the thoughts and memories of the old life alive.

Sequoyah began to record his thoughts and feelings in a notebook. The pages piled up as he traveled through the Southwest. After he had been gone for years, the Cherokees sent a search party to find their lost genius. The riders combed the countryside for weeks until they met a man who had been riding with Sequoyah. "He sleeps the sleep of death," the man reported. Sequoyah's notebooks were never found.

The Cherokees lived on in the Western territory until 1906, when the nation merged with the new state of Oklahoma. To this day land is held in trust by the United States government for the

Cherokees in Tahlequah, Oklahoma. There is also a reservation in North Carolina inhabited by descendants of Cherokees who refused to emigrate between 1839 and 1840.

Though few people read and write in Cherokee anymore, Sequoyah's syllabary means that the Cherokee language will be around for a long time. To honor him, his name has been given to a type of tree that will also be around a long time, the sturdy giant sequoia redwood that grows in the western forests of California. Another memorial, a statue of the great Cherokee, stands in Statuary Hall at the United States Capitol, the only one of an American Indian in the hall.

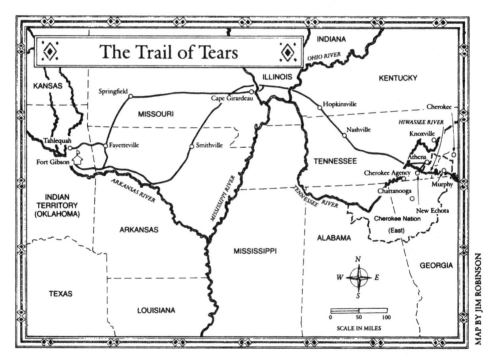

Suggested Reading

Bealer, Alex W. *Only the Names Remain: The Cherokees and the Trail of Tears*. Boston: Little, Brown & Company, 1972.

Bleeker, Sonia. *The Cherokee: Indians of the Mountains*. New York: William Morrow & Company, 1952.

Collier, Peter. *When Shall They Rest?: The Cherokee's Long Struggle with America*. New York: Holt, Rinehart & Winston, 1973.

Johnston, Johanna. *The Indians and the Strangers*. New York: Dodd, Mead & Company, 1972.

Josephy, Alvin M., Jr. *The Patriot Chiefs*. New York: Viking Press, 1961.

ADVANCED READING:

Forman, Grant. *Sequoyah*. Norman, OK: University of Oklahoma Press, 1938.

Van Every, Dale. *The Disinherited*. New York: William Morrow & Co., 1966.